My Time Will Come

The True Story of Abuse, Persevrance, and Love

Anna M. Haines

OWL
PUBLISHING

Owl Publishing, LLC.
www.owlpublishinghouse.com

ISBN:
978-1-949929-61-4 (paperback)
978-1-949929-62-1 (hardcover)

Library of Congress Control Number: In Process

Dedication:

To my husband, Noah, who has always been my support system, and who has constantly accepted me as I am. To my sons, Colin and Logan, who have taught me the true meaning of love, miracles, and motherhood. To everyone who has ever lost a loved one, endured hardship and challenges in their life, may they find understanding, compassion, identity, and true self.

Acknowledgements

I want to give special thanks to Noah, Colin, and Logan for their love, help, and support. They have made my life complete.

I also want to give a special tribute to Melanie, my sister, who died tragically after committing suicide at a young age. To Camille, my mother-in-law, who died of Alzheimer's Disease much too soon and way before her time. I cannot express enough admiration and gratitude to both of you for having such an impact on my life. I miss you both very, very much.

Preface

My Time Will Come follows a series of struggles, unraveling like a mouse maze that often felt inescapable. It is an account of my experiences and struggle with sexual abuse, a dysfunctional family life, the devastating loss of my sister by suicide, and the challenges of being an identical twin.

As one route of the maze was navigated, another always seemed to crop up. The hardships continued with my thirteen-year ordeal to conceive amidst frustrating, often failed attempts at pregnancy, all of which ultimately resulted in in-vitro fertilization. After losing and experiencing the wrenching pain of that loss of my twin babies due to their prematurity, my second set of twins, born successfully, albeit still prematurely, was in a way a miraculous light at the end of the tunnel. The turmoil, as it so often does, continued though, as I coped with my son's medical issues after his early birth.

The personal journey resumes with my unexpected diagnosis of cancer—Stage 3 Non-Hodgkin's Lymphoma—through many twists and turns of combating the disease, coupled with the irony of an untimely misdiagnosis, and process of rigorous chemotherapy treatment.

I hope to be inspirational in telling this story of hope, persistence, and motivation and of finding spirituality, unequaled love, and inner strength. This is a story of refusing to succumb to despair, depression. It's a story about not ever giving up.

I have encountered many books that touch on sexual abuse, suicide, infertility, cancer, and spirituality, but I have tried here to envelop these topics, and to bring them together as personally as I could. This memoir can be described as a little morsel to satisfy a craving for each of those elements. Like the mouse trapped in the maze on the hunt, he is not only searching for an escape but also a tidbit; a tiny taste of cheese to keep him going.

In writing my story, I hope to uncover and reveal the secrets of my past. Not only to expose the stories, but also to release them, and in so doing, help anyone who feels alone, thinks no one cares, and to give encouragement and hope. In the process, I am able to finally tell my story, which is a critical step in my growth and healing. I have always handled these aspects of my life alone, but it is time to say them aloud.

I am not looking for recognition. My only desire by telling my story is that it will give me peace and allow me to close this chapter of my life. In so doing, I will endeavor to help others in need of finding themselves.

One

When I was twelve years old, everything changed. My dad whispered to me one day, "Come with me, I have something to show you." Taking me down into his basement workshop, he went directly to a storage cubbyhole. Amid the disarray and clutter of discarded, tinkered parts, he carefully pulled out a tin canister hidden in the back, well out of sight. Tucked inside was a collection of well-worn, folded up newspaper clippings and a stack of cards. Calmly, he handed me the cards and, flipping through each one, explained, "This is what men and women do." The cards contained graphic pictures of naked men and women engaging in sexual intercourse, caught in the most provocative and explicit of acts.

That was the first time. He looked at me and murmured, "This is our secret; don't tell anyone. Not even Mom."

He excused himself, leaving to go back upstairs and telling me only to, "stay here for a while and look at the cards," as if there was something I could get from them. I stood frozen in fear, as my confusion reverberated through the silence. Uncomfortable and ashamed, I could feel a gut-wrenching, sickening feeling rise from the pit of my stomach. I stared straight ahead to avoid looking at the cards in front of me. I focused my attention instead on the recently disturbed layers of dust caught in the rays of the afternoon sun.

The musty smell of oil and grass lingered in the air as time stood still. Trepidation weighed heavily as I was left wondering, "How long is long enough?" It was as if I was rooted to the spot, caught waiting for that unspecified moment where I could finally do what I wanted— escape this sudden calamity.

That first time was followed by more—more explicit articles, more newspaper clippings of adults promoting sexual intercourse with their children, and more of my dad's insistence that , "There is nothing to be ashamed of; look, everyone does it." Always at the end of every "session," he would repeat, "Don't tell anyone; it's our little secret," and "If you tell, Mom won't believe you, and you will get blamed."

The progression spiraled as he explained what private parts were while touching my vagina and developing breasts. He would pull out his penis, exposing himself, and asking me to touch it, saying, "I will teach you; I will show you how." He had an unrelenting, matter-of-fact way of talking, touching, and encouraging me to participate.

There was an arrogance to his approach—a belief that he was teaching me lessons and his behavior was therefore justified. His moral compass was broken, and the question of right or wrong remained unasked, at least out loud, at least for him. Two to three times a week, he would get me alone, and the exploitation would continue, his actions and expectations ever more brazen and daring.

One of my first memories of Boris, who at the time I thought of as my step-father, was when I was around three years old. We were driving from Brandon, Manitoba to Vancouver, British Columbia in his beat-up 1950s Volkswagen, which he had just converted into a camper for the move. One moment in particular sticks out for me, as Boris pulled over at a roadside food truck and asked if I wanted some homemade fries. I lined up apprehensively next to him, aware suddenly, that the man I was with was a stranger, and that I was alone with him in this unfamiliar crowd.

I was shrinking into myself, timidly carrying the heaping basket of fries to an empty, wooden picnic table that Boris indicated. Sensing my uncertainty, he put me at ease by calmly chitchatting, suggesting I try vinegar on my fries. With such a simple gesture, a moment of paternal teaching, he was able to break through, to make me feel special. Suddenly, this man, a stranger, didn't seem so threatening or so intimidating. Stopping for that treat at the side of the road was just the beginning of our mutual trust.

Later on, Boris was the one who taught me how to ride a bike. He took the training wheels off and raced beside me down the quiet neighborhood streets, steadying the bike when it wobbled. I remember the rush of excitement as second nature took over, and I suddenly had control of this metal contraption underneath me. I could ride, and he was right there with me.

On my seventh birthday, I was gifted a drawing set complete with paper templates for tracing an array of Disney characters: Dumbo the Elephant, Gumby and Pokey, Snow White and The Seven Dwarfs, seemingly anything I wanted. My joy was immediate, and I stretched out on the floor, studiously tracing the characters. In the background, Boris strummed his guitar to the Johnny Cash song emanating from the radio. I was intent on doing my best and meticulous in my efforts. It was only when I was fully pleased with my work that I would hold it up for Boris's approval. It was his praise that I was waiting for, and his praise that turned each sketch into a true accomplishment, causing me to beam with pride.

I was very young, and I didn't remember my biological father. With beaming pride, moments of conspiratorial adventure, and fatherly guidance, I came to accept Boris not only as a stepfather but as my Dad.

$\mathcal{T}wo$

I cannot tell this story of the events that shaped me without first describing the family that shaped those events—how I came to be and those that surrounded me in my early years.

My maternal Grandfather is American, and my Grandmother, Canadian. Long divorced, my Grandfather settled in the Seattle, Washington area, and my Grandmother moved to Edmonton, Alberta, meaning we had roots and connections on either side of the Canadian border. My biological father's family has largely remained a mystery to me.

I was born on December 24, 1961, in Calgary, Alberta, together with my identical twin. My name is Anna, and my twin sister is Tess. I have an older brother, Billy, and two younger sisters, Melanie and Helen.

Billy was born on August 31, 1957, to a different father. My mother was 15 years old when she found herself unexpectedly pregnant and was unceremoniously kicked out of her house. Not only was she underage, she soon learned that Billy's father was married, and that she had been an unwitting participant in an extramarital affair. With neither family willing to offer support, she was to raise Billy on her own.

Four years later, Tess and I were born. Our biological father, Peter, was my mother's first cousin on her mother's side. Peter was an alcoholic and physically and mentally abusive, and life with him was an unyielding assault. We lived in fear of the rare occasion when he was home and would resort to battering my Mom and asserting his control in a drunken stupor. Melanie, my sister, was the last child to be fathered by Peter, born September 15, 1963.

For the first few years of my life, it seemed we were constantly on the road. We left Calgary for Seattle, only to return again before a stint in Brandon, Manitoba. By the time my youngest sister, Helen, was born on August 27, 1966, we had finally settled in Vancouver, British Columbia.

Helen was Boris's only biological child amongst the five of us, but growing up we were led to believe he had fathered us all. It wasn't a difficult leap to make as we were all too young to remember life before he came around. It wasn't until years later we would find out the truth. Once my mother and Peter divorced there was no further communication, no child support, and no relationship. With my actual biological father out of the picture until today, there was an open void, a need for that kind of bond, that Boris was easily able to slip into.

The first few tumultuous years seemed to start calming down when I was about 2 ½ . It was then that my mother found the strength to leave Peter, freeing herself and her children from the throes of his abuse.

Shortly thereafter, my mother met Boris. Boris' relationship with my mother didn't solve all of our problems, of course. They both struggled with the overwhelming financial burden of supporting four children, and it was that ongoing struggle of making ends meet that influenced my parents' decision to cross the border into the U.S. and relocate to Seattle.

Mom and Dad rented the first available house they found, unaware that they had moved into a predominantly Black neighborhood. Tess and I were equally oblivious to the racial dynamics in our new community, focusing our excitement on the school playground situated just up the block the next day. After so much turmoil, we finally had moments of carefree abandon, running back and forth across the playground, free to explore as much as we wanted.

When other children arrived on the playground, though, it was clear we weren't welcome. We were almost instantly ostracized, met with glaring stares of both hostility and indifference. It was easier in those moments for Tess and I to acquiesce to our own apprehension and run back home.

In those days, racial integration was unheard of, and our presence had disturbed the tense racial segregation that was the norm in the community. Later that same night, Billy came home battered and bruised with a bloody nose. My stunned mother couldn't mask her concern as she tried to figure out what had happened. Billy simply replied, "I got into a fight."

I learned later that Billy had used a racial slur in a confrontation with some of the neighborhood children Tess and I had encountered on the playground. Without a full understanding of race, without knowing the long and complicated history of the neighborhood we found ourselves in, we were trying our best to navigate a situation we couldn't come close to comprehending. And for Billy, that had meant defending his sisters.

By the end of that week, our parents were too fearful of our current situation to stay put and we packed up our measly belongings and headed back to Calgary. As we attempted to leave, we took a wrong turn, as we had never gotten to know the area. Lost, my Dad rolled down his window at a traffic light to ask for directions to the highway. A friendly stranger obliged and mapped out a route for us. Unbeknownst to us though, he intentionally gave us directions that led us deeper into a rough neighborhood and away from where we wanted to go.

The intense barrage of slurs and glares increased as we drove in circles in this unknown neighborhood. I sat stunned and silent in the back seat, holding my breath until we finally righted ourselves and headed in the direction of the interstate. As we left Seattle behind, I was left to wrestle with that first experience with racial tension, a concept that I still couldn't fully understand, that still left me with a distinct feeling of being out of place, of feeling entirely foreign.

Three

By the time Tess and I were starting kindergarten, the family had settled in Vancouver. Since Helen was a newborn, and Melanie, a toddler, it fell to Billy to walk us to Sir Charles Elementary School. Billy was four years older, at the ripe old age of 9 was already tired of taking care of his little sisters, who from his perspective were mostly there to steal his toys and smudge his precious Superman comic. So every morning, as soon as the three of us rounded the corner and were out of my mother's line of sight Tess and I were on our own.

Tess and I were fine on our own, though. We couldn't have been more identical physically, with only a lone birthmark and a slight height difference between us, and our mother fully embraced our similarities—dressing us the same and equipping us with the same haircut. Far more than appearance, from our earliest days we had come to fully rely on each other.

Like so many sets of twins, from the time we could talk, Tess and I had our own "language." And frankly, talking to each other, incomprehensible to anyone around us was all that we needed. Other people were intimidating, requiring social skills we hadn't yet developed and a trust that the world hadn't earned. We spent our days clinging to each other in the hidden confines of the cloakroom, trying not to let anyone in.

Our kindergarten teacher did nothing to help draw us out of our shell. An older woman focused on propriety and maintaining order, her principle role in my early life seemed to be belittling me in front of my peers. Schools in those days put an emphasis on public displays of obedience, requiring students to stand and answer questions, and every time I would try to do so I was met with a firm instance to, "Speak up; I can't hear you," followed by, "Speak clearly; I can't understand you." I would have to repeat myself over and over until she was satisfied and had berated me enough. I had started my school career already shy, and those early humiliations were only causing me to crawl further and further inside my shell, allowing only Tess in.

After those first terrifying weeks of kindergarten, being left to walk alone by our brother only to be scolded by our teacher, Tess and I were finally befriended by a classmate, Margaret, who quickly became the only person we allowed near us. She lived down the block from us on Nanaimo Street, and being an only child, needed us just as much as we needed her. The three of us were inseparable, and she was the only person who would come to my rescue under my teacher's harsh reprimand, even at her own expense. She would stand up with me, answering for me and listening, really listening, to what I had to say.

Four

Tess and I had gotten each other through that first year of school, but when we moved on to first grade, we were split up and put into different classrooms. It was school policy that twins be divided after kindergarten to establish individuality. Which, despite my initial trepidation, ended up being exactly what happened.

Having my friend Margaret in my class gave me an ally, someone to rely on now that I was on my own, and she even ended up convincing me to join the choir with her. Even though singing has never been my forte, the camaraderie of those practice sessions brought me even further out of my shell, as I found a new comfort and sense of joy in the all-consuming rhapsody of music.

While extra-curriculars were giving me an outlet and a place to thrive, academics still were holding me back. I was failing language and arithmetic, and my reading and spelling marks were not much better. While it had at first been less noticeable because of my shyness and general reticence to speak, it was becoming clearer and clearer that I had a speech impediment, which was starting to hold me back at school.

Luckily, I was able to start working with a speech therapist who instructed me on the correct technique, the curled-up roll of the tongue for "R," and the hissing sound for "S." I practiced how to roll my tongue and articulate words by slowing down to get the right pronunciation, all for the reward of a few Tootsie rolls at the end of each session . By the time I "graduated" from speech therapy a few months later, my speech was clearer, my "Rs" sharper, and I left our last session grinning ear-to-ear with a full bag of Tootsie Rolls under my arm as a result—the ultimate reward.

As I found my footing at school, my life outside of school also gave me glimmers of joy as I found more and more independence. It was around this same time that I was allowed to walk to the corner store by myself for the first time. I kept my hands in my pocket with the jingling coins, fiddling with them in my fingers, anticipating all of the penny candy I would be able to buy.

When I got to the store, I stood on my tippy toes to peer over the counter at the display, finally settling on my favorite, a pack of candy cigarettes. I loved them less for the flavor, which was mostly just a vague sweetness, but the fact that they were a way to play at being a grown-up as I walked back to the house, putting one in my mouth and puffing away—the height of candy sophistication.

One year we went to the Pacific National Exhibition, an amusement park on Hastings Street in Vancouver. There were throngs of people milling about, and at some point, Tess and I looked up and realized that we had been separated from the rest of the family. Clutching each other's hands, we managed to navigate ourselves back to the parking lot, and to find the family car. Sometimes it helped to be withdrawn, as my shyness left me with nothing else to do but observe the path we had taken.

It took hours for the rest of the family to return, as my mother rushed up to us in quickly subsiding panic. They had been searching high and low for us throughout the park and were shocked that we'd been right there waiting the whole time. She had been petrified; her only thought was we had been kidnapped. Tess and I didn't get to go on any rides that day. As the early evening rolled around and exhaustion set in on everyone's part, we decided that was enough to end our outing for the day.

When I was about 7, we moved to Abbotsford, B.C. where we rented a house on multiple acres in the countryside right off of Old Yale Road. Formerly a working farm, the land was expansive and isolated, far from even the closest neighbors. Boris had dreams of revitalizing the farm, and purchased a couple of young calves to get himself started. Unfortunately, one early morning, he awoke to find one of the calves had frozen to death, succumbing to the frigid temperatures overnight. She was, it seemed, a reckless calf, having escaped the warm confines of the shed. Soon after, the second calf died of the same fatal mistake. Having spent all of the money set aside on those two cows, Boris had no other choice but to go and find employment.

He got hired at a small-time dairy operation as a milk delivery driver. After hurting his back one day, he came to Tess and I in secret to ask if we wanted to skip school and go and help deliver milk on his route. We jumped at the chance to miss school and eagerly waited for his return with the fully stocked delivery truck. It was a fun adventure for us, riding in the old-fashioned milk truck and jumping on and off when we had to make deliveries.

Our job was to collect the discarded glass milk jugs placed outside of the customer's front door and exchange them for the new order, running back and forth with more glee than the task may have warranted. Of course, the novelty wore off by the end of the first day, as we collapsed, exhausted into bed that night, our little 7-year old bodies wrecked from work usually done by someone at least a little older.

As tired as I was though, I fell asleep with a smile on my face. It had been the best reason to miss school: I'd gotten to spend the whole day with Boris. We'd topped off the day with an assortment of well-deserved goodies: ice cream fudge sundaes, chocolate milk, strawberry shortcake dessert cups, that we'd grabbed from the supermarket and eaten in the back of the milk truck, our legs dangling off the sides.

In addition to all us kids, and the occasional ill-fated cow, the farm in Abbotsford was also home to a Rhodesian Ridgeback named Spot. He spent his days in the carport; where he was intended to serve as a guard dog, though he never quite got the hang of that role. He seemed much more interested in chewing through shoes, or whatever else was lying around.

One day, in a rare flash of rage, Boris took a long rope and tied it to Spot's collar. He jumped in his car and forced Spot to run alongside the car at high speed. Driving up and down our front street, he kept up and didn't stop until Spot collapsed out of pure exhaustion. Billy ran screaming behind the truck, pleading for him to stop. By the time he stopped though, Boris's usual steely calm had returned as he untied Spot, saying only, "Maybe now he'll learn."

Eventually, our Aunt Sue moved into a dilapidated, make-shift shack on our property with our three cousins. She had just left her husband, and our house was the only place that they had to go. As difficult as their situation must have been, I was mostly excited to have a new playmate in my cousin Gayle. Engrossed in girl-talk, gossip, boys, and school, we would sit cross-legged on her front porch, sneaking glances over our shoulders to ensure our privacy.

One summer's day, we snuck into the garden and picked rhubarb to eat as a surreptitious snack. Gayle had grabbed a container filled with sugar from the kitchen, and we sat hidden behind shrubs dipping and munching, and puckering at the sour taste of raw rhubarb. My excitement dissolved moments later when Aunt Sue discovered our hiding place. I sat there sheepish and shamefaced, while she reprimanded us for eating from the garden, and in a rare candid moment shared the real source of her concern: "You know we barely have enough food to go around!"

In stealing the rhubarb, along with many other misadventures, I was a follower, going along with whatever Gayle suggested. We were always exploring, and always going places we weren't supposed to. On one such occasion, we even ended up sneaking onto a construction site. It was already dark, and the place was deserted, already locked up for the night. A sense of calm washed over me there in the quiet as we squeezed through a small tear in the temporary fencing and surveyed our surroundings.

Construction was well underway, and massive underground steel water main pipes littered the site ready for installation. The site made for a perfect backdrop for our make believe, and Gayle and I bounded headfirst, intent on crawling through the dark recesses of our imaginary tunnels. Laughing and joking, we heedlessly scurried through until I sliced my knee open on an exposed bolt. The pain wasn't the only problem here—I was going to have to come up with a lie to explain the rip in my jeans and the blood-soaked stain. I certainly wasn't going to admit that we had been up to no good.

When we got home, I was able to excuse it with a casual "I slipped and fell." After a couple of days, the deep gash wouldn't stop bleeding, and I knew the severity of my injury would betray the meager excuse I had given. I was panicked to discover blood seeping through my jeans one day while doing the ironing. On the pretense of putting away the laundry, I snuck into my bedroom to change my jeans, hoping and praying that Mom would not catch on, probe deeper, and question me. Even then, my fear of getting in trouble had already been ingrained, and secrecy had already set in.

Five

My mother met Boris in 1964 when she worked for him at a janitorial company he owned in Calgary, Alberta. She was already divorced from my biological father at that point, and was on her own with four kids, doing everything she could to make ends meet.

Once Boris came into our lives, it seemed like we were always on the go. I spent countless nights in the backseat of the car, watching the moon follow us, wondering how it was always there. No matter how far we traveled, it never strayed, like a lifelong friend lying in wait.

When we would cross the border into the U.S., Boris, who by then I called Dad, would completely fill the underside of the backseat with liquor from the duty-free shop. With each bump, we could hear the precarious clinking of the bottles as they jolted and jarred. Holding their breath, my Mom and Dad prayed that none would break and fill the car with the unmistakable odor of whiskey. Once we got close to the border, we were told to lie down and pretend to be asleep. If we were sleeping, my parents hoped, the agents wouldn't want to disturb us, and we could make our way back to Canada with their stash undiscovered beneath us.

❦

There was always somewhere new for us to be, and something for us to adjust to. I have a vague memory of spending a couple of days at a nudist colony around the age of three. I remember being told to undress, and that my mother said we couldn't keep our clothes on. There was no explanation given, but I knew enough to be bashful, to feel strange taking my clothes off when we weren't alone. It was only at Mom's insistence that we dubiously ran buck-naked to play. Returning to the motel room, my Mom noticed there was no tub, only a shower stall. As we were too young to be left unattended, she allowed Boris to get in the shower naked with my sisters and me. I remember standing in the shower and, with the innocence of a child, grabbed hold of my Dad's penis and asked, "What's that?" Not disapproving, and not in the least bit uncomfortable with my actions, he smiled and replied, "It's called a penis." I asked a couple more curious questions before I eventually got bored. It would be a long time before I understood the weight of that exchange.

I remember very early on asking my mother , "Why do I have to write "Boiko" on my school supplies when our last name is Barnes?" The name felt like it didn't belong to me, sounding strange as I tripped over it's pronunciation, and as I found myself constantly misspelling what was suddenly supposed to be my name. My mother offered very little explanation only that my name was Boiko, and that I would use it.

I assumed my new name, and it wasn't until I was sixteen years old and went to get my driver's license that I realized my name was not actually Boiko. The name change had not been officially filed and was never legal. My name was Barnes, as I had insisted on all those years ago.

In those days, there was never quite enough money to go around, and we had to make do with hand-me-downs and minimal extras. It was just the way things were though, and we barely noticed until Aunt Sue and our cousins came to visit one year. She had gotten back on her feet since the days she stayed on our property, and was newly dating a man named Barry.

One night, Barry showed up at our door, having just returned from a business trip. Introductions were hurried, but all us kids could focus on were the bags he was clutching—filled to the brim with the newest toys and clothes. As if he didn't even notice the other kids in the room, Barry shouted to our cousins to come and open their gifts. We watched as our cousins ripped open the presents in unbridled excitement. These kids had been staying with us just months before, and here they were surrounded by good fortune and gifts I couldn't have dreamed of. It was my first experience with jealousy and resentment, and that gnawing feeling wasn't going to go away any time soon.

After two years of relative stability in Abbotsford, we were uprooted again in May of 1970, only a month before I was supposed to finish third grade. This time, we found ourselves in Tacoma, Washington, and Tess and I were sent to Fernhill Elementary School to finish off the year.

As had quickly become the norm for us, we were enrolled in different classrooms, and one day, my teacher thought up an "experiment": she wants Tess and I to switch classrooms to see if anyone could tell us apart. In the moment, I was excited to see if anyone would notice. It lasted an hour or so as Tess and I changed classrooms and were told to act like each other. Well, my teacher's theory was right—no one noticed. As excited as I had been, being faced with the fact that I was interchangeable with someone else, even Tess, was a harsh reality that would take a while to sink in.

As time went on, being a twin was starting to lose its luster. Everywhere we went, we were lumped together as one—"the twins", our individual names practically irrelevant. There was, at least to my mind, a constant comparison, and I was always coming up short—I was the secondary twin. When anyone spoke to me, they assumed I was Tess, and people seemed more prone to using Tess's name over mine. I wanted everyone to know me for me, not just as Tess's other half.

Standing next to each other, no one could resist a litany of comments on how much we looked alike. It became quite monotonous to have the minute details of our appearance scrutinized, constantly getting the same questions over and over. The sisterly bond is irreplaceable—but the experience of being a twin, that was something I would have happily traded away.

Every day at school, when the lunch bell rang, I would wander the school grounds, listlessly observing the scurried commotion and the unabashed frolicking of kids released from their classrooms, breaking off into their cliques. I grew quite accustomed to spending time alone, as even Tess was off somewhere blending in with the crowd.

The monotony was punctured one day by a teacher coming out of the school with a football in hand. He was one of the friendliest, as well as the youngest teachers in the school, and we all looked up to him, so he was met enthusiastically when he held the ball above his head shouting, "Who wants to play football!?" We all raced to spread out across the field to play. The teacher said, "Okay, I'm going to toss the football; let's see who can catch it." He threw a long, hard pass, and the football steadily swirled as it sliced through the air. The distance was impressive, and I tried to maintain focus on the ball, as it glided right into my outstretched hands. Never having touched a football before, I had miraculously caught it without even the slightest fumble. The teacher shouted out, "That was pretty good, great catch!" I was beaming with pride and for the first time since we had moved, disappointed when the lunch bell rang, ending recess and the football game along with it.

With the exception of my momentary athletic glory, I had mostly given up on coming out of my shell or initiating friendships. That was until one morning, walking by myself to school, a girl around the same age came up, and said, "Hi, I'm Sally - can I walk with you?" Outgoing enough to puncture even my cold exterior, she was small, and dressed in worn-ill fitting clothes that signaled a layer of hardship beyond her sparkling self-confidence. She went on to say, "No one talks to me," and when I asked her why, she said, "It's because of my hand." She explained that both she and her older brother had a congenital disability colloquially called claw hand. I wasn't bothered, and from that day on I had a friend. We walked to school every day, and her brother joined us soon after. We all had our outcast status in common, and while we went our separate ways when we got to school, those moments of companionship to and from were invaluable.

25

Money was tight, and my Mom and Dad were constantly looking for ways to earn extra money. Our time was filled with odd jobs—from delivering phone books, to retrieving discarded furniture, to babysitting, and selling Avon products. Once in a while when we could afford a treat, we would go to a chocolate factory in Seattle. It was located in a beautiful old building in historic downtown, where we could stare through the glass window and the array of sweets. Upon entering the store, my Mom and Dad would charm their way into enough free samples for all of us. All of us then lunged savoring the creamy, rich, succulent taste of the sweet chocolate. Smiling ruefully, they would thank the clerk and we'd scurry away, not having made a single purchase.

The only extracurricular activity Tess and I did outside of choir was the Brownies Girl Scouts. My mother had been pressured by an overly pushy Supervisor into signing us up, and forking over a set of fees that we really shouldn't have been paying. Thrilled at first, my Mom's complaining about the cost quickly put a damper on my excitement. Not pleased with putting out the money she didn't have, she had no choice but to save face. After all, she had her pride, reputation mattered, and she cared what people thought, so she wasn't going to pull us out now. As shy as I was, I took to the activities and challenges easily, if not to the social aspect. I quickly earned a merit badge, but my time as a Brownie was cut short by our next impending move.

At the end of 4th Grade, we moved once more, back into Canada to a village 200 km east of Calgary, Alberta. My Dad's parents owned a farm on the outskirts of town that encompassed hundreds of acres of land. It was a self-sustaining farm which raised cattle, livestock, pigs, and chickens. The move was the first time I had ever met my Dad's parents, who I couldn't even bring myself to call Grandparents—they were strangers to me.

Farm life was very unfamiliar to me. There wasn't any indoor plumbing; instead we had an outhouse and a cast iron bathtub in the yard. My Mom collected rainwater in barrels until she had enough to fill the tub. It wasn't until I stepped in the first time that I realized something I should have pieced together already—a rainwater bath is freezing! We each took turns in the tub, turning around when a sibling was bathing to give some semblance of privacy.

I remember one day my Dad's Mom strode purposely down to the chicken coop on a mission and announced, "It's time we had some chicken!" She grabbed a chicken and snapped its neck in one decisive motion, leaving the headless body bouncing across the yard as I watched aghast. The nerves still intact, the twitching and flailing were unrelenting. She chopped off the chicken's feet, rinsed them off, and started munching on them. I stood looking horrified and disgusted and, moments later, surprised by my insolence, she remarked, "Haven't you ate chicken feet before?" Holding the chicken feet out, she asked, "Do you want to try some?" I shook my head in terror, and vehemently answered, "No!" She merely shrugged saying, "Okay, but you don't know what you're missing!"

My Grandparents had a rigid, strenuous routine, and a no-nonsense approach that sometimes erred on the side of abrasive. Mostly out of curiosity, if not a tinge of fear, I wouldn't leave their side, taking an interest in the daily chores and listening attentively to the stories told. I was quickly picking up the basics of farm life—driving the tractor, feeding the livestock, and processing and pasteurizing the milk. I even found out that pigs love to eat coal and would go around digging up the ground in search of coal, to toss it in the pig-pen for them to eat.

Along with my new skills, I was also being brought face to face with the stark realities of life on the farm. I had to walk away crying when I watched a pig get butchered, still squeamish at the sight. The land was also overrun with gophers, and when they popped up from their burrows, shots would inevitably ring out. My dad's explanation was merely, "It's target practice and, besides, the rodents eat and destroy our crops."

Sometimes, I caught glimpses of the gentler, softer side of my grandparents. When my grandfather showed me how to milk a cow, we were accompanied by several stray cats. He flashed a rare smile and explained, "I give them milk, and scraps as well as they're the ones that keep the rats away. In return, I look after them, and they keep me company too." My grandmother too, had her moments, as I followed her through her vegetable garden she would sneak in lessons on what she had planted, and when she would harvest them. In those moments, she never lost her patience and was not the least bit concerned with how much time had passed.

For reasons that were never explained to me, we didn't stay long, and we were off to Delta, British Columbia before landing back on the farm. This time, the plan was to settle in and eventually take it over. We arrived to find that my Grandfather had purchased a rundown, old railway station that he thought would be a perfect fixer-upper for us to live in. He bragged about how cheap he'd gotten it for, but failed to mention that it was the site of multiple homicides. That fact gave us all the heebie-jeebies, and soured our plan quickly. This was not what my mother had envisioned, and almost as soon as we'd arrived we were back on the road, this time headed back out West to Burnaby, B.C., where I was to start the 6th grade.

Our house on Sprotte Street was located opposite the Twilight Drive-in and, many lazy summer nights, we would sit out on the front porch watching the movies that were visible on the large theater screen. Billy managed to get a job as a short order cook at the drive-in concession, and soon after my Mom and Dad were cleaning the drive-in lot to earn spare cash. Every Friday night and weekends, we all joined in, and row after row we'd pick up all the strewn garbage. Us kids never got paid, and never really expected to, but the prospect of finding money or lost treasures tossed mistakenly on the ground was enough to keep us going. One night, my dad managed to run a speaker over to our house. We had sound and watched the movies for free!

I was a mousy, gangly, and awkward 11-year-old. I was profoundly uncomfortable in my own skin, and never thought I was pretty, especially with my thick lensed-glasses and long hair, which fell flat down my back. The most striking thing about me was a single streak of natural blonde hair. I had a slight curvature in my spine, and my mom was constantly admonishing me to, "Stand up straight, don't hunch over, and put your shoulders back." More of a tomboy, I never had an inclination to wear dresses or embrace anything I saw as particularly feminine. I wasn't part of the popular crowd, didn't stand out by any means, and my family didn't have the money to afford the kinds of stylish clothing I thought I would need to fit in, which I tried as hard as I could to not let bother me.

Our house, built in the early 1900s had stood empty and in disrepair for quite some time when we arrived. Pulling up, exhausted from the drive, this did not feel like home. We walked through the back door and were greeted with filth, grime on every surface, and a foul stench accompanying a heaping pile of debris and trash that only a shovel could undo. Forced to make friends fast, we went knocking on neighbors' doors until my mom could find anyone to help. We were lucky enough to find Norm and Janet Russett, who took pity on us and allowed us to sleep on their living room floor that first night.

Eventually, we would make it livable, though it remained rather shoddy, with dated, dark green wood siding and a covered front porch overlooked the obscure, shaded front yard. A weeping willow tree, was the focal point of the yard, with its gnarled, drooping limbs spreading rampantly. The backyard out for a quarter acre, with an array of fruit trees scattering the property. A separate garage, at the end of the narrow, oil-slicked driveway, had a double-entry door with a separate side entrance door to the yard, and an adjoining shed. Unkempt and neglected overgrowth ran the course of the driveway adjacent to the lane.

Upon entering our house, you immediately noticed the narrow, enclosed staircase ascending to the attic, with two rooms, one on each side. When you walked into the small living room, compact in size, the original fireplace jutted one wall, and the couch was placed opposite in front of the window. The tight space past the console television brought you into the kitchen. The outdated sink ran alongside the inside wall, directly in the path of the back door. A large table placed in the center of the room was the only obvious choice since there was not a separate dining room. As you turned to the right entering the small hallway, the sole bathroom was on the left. Tiny, it held a toilet, a washbasin, and a claw-foot tub. Possibly the worst flaw of the house was a small window above the toilet, with full view of the stairs, and occasionally, of our neighbor Norm coming up them.

In a welcome change from many of our previous living situations, we were only two to a room, with Tess and I sharing the bedroom in the attic, Helen and Melanie on the other side of the stairwell and Billy in the bedroom opposite my parents' room.

Our financial luck was starting to turn around in those days. We purchased a brand-new, candy red mini-bike, and immediately started competing against each other. Our route traversed through the yard, down the driveway, cutting through the lane, and then back into the yard. On one occasion, hitting the stretch of open yard, I opened up the throttle and bombed down the yard. We were looking after a friend's dog, and had tied him to a tree while outside. Before I knew it, the dog had bolted straight out in front of me, and in a split-second, I was hanging by the rope! Unable to release the throttle, the forward momentum kept me suspended in midair. The sudden burst of the engine roaring sent the dog running scared, and as he tried to escape his actions kept the rope taut. All the commotion caught my Mom and Dad's attention, and after a brief pause they rushed over and yanked me off the mini-bike. I collapsed to the ground writhing in pain and gasping for breath.

Rushing me to the doctor, he said, "You're very lucky the rope didn't penetrate any deeper." The rope burn was too severe to wrap and, extremely self-conscious, I had to face my classmates the next day and explain that what looked like I had tried to hang myself was nothing more than an accident involving a bike, a dog, and a rope.

Another time while out riding the mini-bike, I'd cut alongside the front sidewalk to head back through the lane. At that same moment, a police car happened to come up our street. Spotting me, he flashed his lights on and wanted me to stop. I darted, ripped into the lane, and reached the dense canopy of our backyard before the cop had a chance to see my retreat. Turning off the mini-bike, I sat quietly in my hiding spot peering through the thick foliage. I watched as the policeman parked his patrol car in the lane, got out, and ambled into our backyard. Avoiding detection, the policeman grew puzzled by my vanishing act and returned to his car. Unfortunately, in a mere matter of minutes, he was back in our yard, and this time he was accompanied by my mom and dad. I sat motionless in hiding until I heard my mom say, "She was just out here; where has she gone?" With her calling out my name, I had no choice but to reveal myself. Naturally, the cop was annoyed, and in a gruff tone said, "Don't let me see you riding on the front boulevard again; it's illegal. Next time don't try and hide," as he plucked and handed over a fine.

When Billy was around 16 years of age, he called the police to report our neighbors across the lane were growing pot and agreed to give a statement. Billy and I were the only ones at home when the police arrived, and made themselves comfortable in the living room to ask for details. The formality of the situation and the seriousness of the two policemen as they took their notes was too much for me. My nerves kicked in, and I let out a giggle. Both officers shot me a look of stern disapproval and asked, "Is this a joke - what are you laughing at?" My outburst was enough to cast doubt on Billy's story, and they left assuming we had made the whole thing up. Billy was indignant that I had ruined his moment of heroism, growling, "What's the matter with you? You could have got us into a whole heap of trouble." Growing more irritated at my lack of response he shouted, "I'm serious; they thought I was making it up - don't do that again!"

Much to my own chagrin though, that would not be the only time my nervous laugh would get me into trouble. I would often ride Tess's much more social coattails into invitations to friends' houses, including, once, her new friend Nina. Tess and I sat in the kitchen while we waited for Nina to finish up helping her Mom. I was always nervous in new situations—and always laughed when I was nervous, so soon we were both in a fit of uncontrollable laughter. Unable to stop, we eventually had tears streaming down our face from laughing so hard. Even the sight of Nina's obvious annoyance, as she stood over us with her hands on her hips, could do little to curb our hysteria.

Six

At 12-years-old, I was quite naive, and thought for sure it was all my fault. The secret I kept, and I didn't tell. My Mom, preparing dinner one night, asked Helen to go and tell Dad supper was ready. Her quiet, soft tread startled us as she interrupted our workshop "learning session." Dad, taken off-guard, quickly turned his back to her, tucked his penis back into his pants, and hastily did his zipper up. Once done, he nonchalantly turned around pretending to be preoccupied with sorting out his tools. Unassumingly, he asked, "What do you want?" and Helen said, "It's supper." My Dad, exhibiting no signs of outward discomfort, said, "Go upstairs; I'll be there in a minute." It was a close call, too close, and I wonder even now if Helen had an incomprehensible, first-hand view. Being only eight years old, she would not have clued into what she saw.

It wasn't long before Dad brazenly invaded the sanctity of my bedroom. I shared a bed with my twin, and very late at night he would appear, quietly shaking me awake. He would whisper in my ear, "Go downstairs to the basement, lay on the couch, and wait for me. I'll be right down. Don't make any noise, and don't turn the lights on. If anyone wakes up, just tell them you had to go to the bathroom." It is staggering, unbelievable how no one overheard and, never woke up, considering Tess was in the same bed, Helen and Melanie were right across the stairwell, and even Billy slept in his room directly across from my parents' bedroom.

There was only one time my Mom awoke and, puzzled by my Dad's absence, called out to him. Panicked, he stood silently looking out our bedroom window. Reading his facial expression, I could tell he was pondering and was trying to come up with an excuse for being up in our bedroom. A minute later, he made his way back downstairs, and I could hear him telling Mom, "I thought I heard a noise outside, and I went upstairs to look out the window to see if I could find anything."

My Dad took on the role of "instructor" to teach me about sex, and on one couch session would use massage as another technique to justify and enhance his actions. He had been a self-taught massage therapist at one point in time and did his practice from home. I still remember him taking a client into his private massage room, closing the door to prevent any interruptions, and an hour or so later coming out smiling - the woman I mean.

Using his massage oils, he would gingerly massage my body starting at my toes and work his way up. He would express his confidence by saying, "This will give you pleasure, and make it more enjoyable." I would lay on the couch motionless and, clad only in pajamas; I would shiver from the cold, half asleep. This night, he finally stopped after noticing that I was shaking uncontrollably and said, "Go back to bed, we'll continue tomorrow night." The next night he had a blanket placed on the couch and, this time with no pretense climbed on top, and penetrated. In discomfort, I managed to make my way back to my bedroom. As I crawled back into bed, I curled up in the fetal position. Lost and alone, I suffered through the violation, the physical pain, and the bleeding. The emotional scar of my virginity taken; left me loathing, ashamed, and broken inside.

Two to three times a week became the routine. He would always try to get me to participate, try new ways, but I would never relent. Quite literally, I was a puppet. Placing me in different positions or taking my hand to encourage participation, he was the puppet master. He controlled the strings, and on release, I would go limp, and do nothing but wait for our session to be over. He took my virginity, my innocence, and my childhood. The abuse was constant, an unrelenting torture of self-gratification on his part. When it was my turn to do supper dishes, he would come up behind me and, after checking to see that no one was in sight, would push and jut himself up against me. His dry humping caused his erection, and, in his excitement, he whispered, "I'll be up to get you tonight."

After a time, I would avoid my Dad, and became quite adept at making sure he didn't have the chance to get me alone. It was becoming quite strained as Dad's frustration of not getting his way led to his growing hostility. His dominance and control weakening, he resorted to complaining to Mom about my so-called insolence. Unable to give the real reason for his disapproval, he invoked dissension and discord and had my Mom siding with him. I was alone in my efforts to protect myself, and my only defense was to stay away, and then I would be safe.

One summer afternoon, my Mom, Dad, and sisters were in the pool. An above-ground pool that easily fit 8 to 10 people. I stood outside the pool watching, not wanting to get into the pool with my Dad present. My Mom called out, "Anna come on, get in the pool," and I answered, "No, I'm okay - I don't want to." She kept insisting, and still, I insisted, "No, I can't - I don't have anything to wear." Unabashed, she replied, "Go to my room and get one of my old bathing suits from the dresser. Try them on; I'm sure one of them will fit." Defeated, I turned and went to her bedroom.

Once in the house and out of sight, I stormed over to her dresser. Yanking out her bathing suits, I flung them on her bed, and in a fury slammed the drawer shut. My anger was boiling over; I silently voiced my contempt. Venting my rage, I continued my rampage and furiously hurled the unwanted bathing suits down on the bed. I had no desire to go to the pool or wear one of my Mom's bathing suits. Still, in a state of loathing, I did not hear my Dad enter the room. Startled, I jumped and, a split second later, stood stock-still to hide my outward display of emotion. In the pretense of trying to help, he picked up one of the bathing suits, and commented, "I don't think this one will fit; your boobs aren't big enough, not yet." Once more, he had managed to get me alone, and while shoving himself against me, he quite joyously fondled my small breasts. The all too familiar words as he said,

"I'll be up to get you tonight."

Defeated, I went back outside, and told Mom, "None of your bathing suits fit," and excused myself.

To this day, I dread anyone coming up behind me, and I will strike out. I even take it as far as holding a door open, so I don't have to go first. It is a habit I will not break.

I kept up my routine - going to school and coming home. It was the start of Grade 8, and I went from elementary school to Windermere Jr. Secondary School.

My Mom, trying to resolve the conflict, the tension at home, would say, "Why don't you do something nice for Dad, just try," and on one occasion, with his birthday coming up said, "Why don't you go wash his car; that would be nice." He had a Cadillac, an old 1960s model, which was his pride and joy. Objecting, I tried in vain to come up with excuse after excuse for not washing his car, but it fell on deaf ears. Sure enough, it wasn't long before my Dad made his way out to the garage. I was caught, cornered, between the devil and the deep blue sea. Approaching me, he spoke in a low, hushed voice and asked, "Why are you washing my car? You know what I want." All the while, he feigned a look of hurt. I stood staring at the floor, not answering, angered that I had been boxed into a corner once more, and the oh-so-common phase came again, "I'll come get you tonight." So much for washing his car!

One afternoon, I got the surprise of my life when I exited school as the dismissal bell rang. Stepping out, a jarring blare of a car horn startled me, and glancing around I spotted Dad parked outside the school. Perplexed, I headed towards him unsure of why he was there. He never picked me up from school! Getting closer, he called out, "Get in, we need to have a talk." My mind racing, I wondered what had happened, and became concerned that something dreadful had occurred. Apprehensively, I opened the passenger door, slipped in, and quietly waited. Not speaking, he reached down under his seat, pulled out my diary, and placed it in my lap. I inwardly groaned, and in horror thought, "Oh no, I'm in trouble now!" I had written everything down and more, and he had found it.

Visible only to the naked eye, I emptied my pent-up frustrations and anger onto paper –deep within the pages of my hidden diary. Daily journals exposing the sexual abuse I was subjected to, and every entry more damaging and incriminating.

My good-natured demeanor replaced with aloofness, and no one noticed the subtle differences. My disposition, already one of being shy and reserved, magnified two-fold. My world turned abruptly to silence, disconnect, and disdain.

Melanie and Helen, on the other hand, had not a care in the world, they were happy-go-lucky. They were being dotted upon and given attention and approval. Envious and jealous, I would write about Melanie calling her, "The Little Princess" as in my eyes, they could do no wrong.

Dad talked for a while, a one-sided conversation, and his final comment was to say, "A word of advice - never write anything down; you might get caught." I listened and, up until now, never wrote anything down again. He wasted no time in snatching back my diary and, intent on destroying the evidence, he threw it away.

Melanie's delicate features were graceful and alluring - her flowing, long, dirty-blonde hair permeated only by her petite stature; her smiling, carefree nature captivating by a gentle and caring disposition. Helen too, long blonde hair and blue eyes - tomboyishly cute, she had a tendency of using her charms to get her way. Helen, being the youngest, had a way of wiggling out of doing chores, and more often than not was spoiled. Even the punishment she would turn into a game, laughing and squirming her way out. Fueled by her rambunctious ways, my Dad was unable to keep his grip long enough and tired of his attempts to subdue her; her punishment soon forgotten. Helen successfully avoided the strap or spanking. Already starting my teenage years, this did not improve my perception of myself. It didn't help when Mom would say, "Stand up straight; stop slouching." I was insecure, had no self-esteem, and the confidence just wasn't there.

I wonder only now - how odd it was that Dad was the one to

stumble upon my diary. You would think it would have been Mom since she was the one to clean our rooms. My diary, tucked way under my bed mattress, was not easily found. Maybe circumstances would have turned out differently if it had been my Mom who had found my diary instead.

As Junior Prom drew near, I braced myself as I noticed a boy during class standing nearby stealing glances at me. Valiantly, he tried to remain inconspicuous, but his actions said otherwise. Busily wringing his hands together, I noticed the beads of perspiration streaming down the pudgy sides of his face. Unsure of what to do with his hands, he shoved them in his pockets and, with all the gumption he could muster, casually sauntered over. A paunchy, burly boy, he wavered, nervously psyching himself up to ask me to the prom. I was disappointed as my hopes of being asked by another boy dashed. Unwilling to hurt his feelings by telling him he wasn't my type, I accepted. My wardrobe barren of any dresses, I begrudgingly wore an ill-fitting, dated, old-fashioned lace dress my Mom plucked from her closet. The embarrassment hit new heights as this boy asked me to dance. Our stilted, awkward attempts were quite noticeable as we both didn't know how to dance. My date started sweating profusely, adding to my discomfort, and repelled by his moist, clammy hands I breathed a sigh of relief when it was finally over.

Our family was very dysfunctional, and we were raised to keep our family life private; our problems stayed behind closed doors. No matter what, you kept the family loyalty; silence was the unspoken code, and no one was to know our family secrets.

The end of school is looming, and a field trip to the local leisure center gave way to anticipation - the opportunity to learn how to swim.

That morning, excitement turned to disappointment as Tess and I both got our period. We sat on the sidelines, and every attempt at getting us in the pool matched with a deliberate cop-out. Our reluctance was not only questioned by our teacher's unfaltering bewilderment, but by my Mom's constant harping when she came to pick us up. It wasn't until the next day I gathered my courage and explained to her why we hadn't gone swimming. Her response was to say, "For Heaven's sake, why didn't you tell me? You could have worn a tampon!" Stupefied, I could only stare as I didn't have the slightest idea what she was talking about; I was only twelve! Exasperated by my apparent confusion, she handed me the box of tampons. Feeling belittled, I asked, "What am I supposed to do with this?" Once more, the embarrassment as it was a repeat of the time when I had started my period and, handing me a sanitary pad and belt, she expected me to know what to do with it! It wasn't a typical bonding Mother/Daughter moment, and I never did learn how to swim.

An outing to the beach one afternoon would bring about a dire, life-changing fear of water. Looking out across the calm, tranquil water, I saw my Mom and Grandmother engaged in conversation way out beyond the shore. Wading through the water, I was eager to join them, and I labored in my pursuit to reach them. As soon as I was nearby, I plummeted down, instantaneously submerged in the deep recesses of the cool water. Unknowingly, I had hit the drop-off point, and with nothing below my feet, I was drowning! Bobbing up and down, I swallowed large amounts of water as I struggled to get some air. Unable to scream or shout, I grew weary and exhausted by my failed attempts to get a breath of air. With my Mom and Grandmother completely oblivious to my predicament, it wasn't until my Grandmother grabbed hold of me, to scold me, said, "Stop fooling around!" that I managed to secure my footing. Since then, I have a fear of deep water, and still, don't know how to swim.

My Dad wasn't a moderate beer or wine drinker and preferred the hard liquor instead. An alcoholic, the long-term alcohol abuse was a matter-of-fact routine we became habituated to every day. His temperament, normally jovial, would turn nasty on a dime if you got him mad. Heated arguments would ensue, and his stance was one of controlled, quiet tolerance of my Mom's accusations. My Mom's fury building with intensity, her loud pitched screaming was unavoidable to hear from the other room. Times like this, we were anxious to find out what the fight was about, so we stayed out of sight, but we were all ears.

A well-known fact we all came to endure was our discipline. We would be warned with the strap, my Dad's belt, to behave. The threat we came to know occurred mostly at bedtime. The day unwinding signaled our bedtime, and my Mom would call out, "It's bedtime; go get ready for bed." Tess and I were not given special treatment or allowed to stay up later because of our age. We'd brush our teeth, get our pajamas on, and return to the living room to say our goodnights. After a bit of difficulty getting us to bed, my Mom would say, "Okay, it's bedtime - now go to bed." With that, we raced up the stairs and jumped into our beds. At the time, my sisters and I shared the same room. A single bed for each of us -one positioned under the window, two along the wall, and the last beside the chimney wall. Still not sleepy, we would lay awake talking about nothing in particular. A few minutes later, the warning came as Mom shouted up, "Go to bed - be quiet now, and go to sleep!" Quite a few times, not heeding her words, Dad would be sent up. Whoever he thought was the last one talking would get the punishment. Dreading his ascent, we would grab hold of our blankets, tightly pulled up, squeeze our eyes shut, and hope it wasn't our turn. As he towered over, he would reach down to yank the covers off, and all the while be tugging at his belt. Angered by our defiance, our struggling only made it worse, and one of us would pay the price. This time, it was my turn as he roughly pulled my pajamas bottoms down, and mercilessly administered several strong lashings across my bare bottom while the pillow muffled my cries. Billy was the only one immune from getting the strap, thus insinuating the double standard.

Even at school, the strap was commonplace and used as a form of discipline. Being sent to the Principal's office, your punishment would consist of a few good lashings with the strap across your open hand. The unmistakable screams of the unfortunate student could be heard reverberating down the halls.

It was commonplace when we went to visit relatives, we were told, "Sit down, be quiet, behave, and don't touch anything." We could not accept any offered food or drink and were told to refuse politely. All the while my Mom and Dad socialized in another room, the five of us would sit in a catatonic state. Conditioned, we understood the repercussions of not behaving. Our relatives thought we were so well-mannered and well-behaved. They complimented us on our exemplary behavior.

A stern look of disapproval was all Mom needed to keep us in line. It was the generation you did what was asked, showed respect or else. By all means, you didn't "mouth off" or talk back unless you wanted a firm slap across the face. When all else failed, Dad handed out the punishment.

The phrase, "Clean house, happy home" sums up my Mom's outlook on life. Her tendency was to stay occupied and fill her days with endless household chores. She did not like conflict, and the perception was if she didn't know about it, then she couldn't be bothered with it. To take it one step further, if she pled ignorance, then all was well. In my eyes, she was beyond approachable.

Our emotional well-being we learned by example. Our upbringing was devoid of any heart-to-heart talks, open communication, confiding or sharing. There was no emotional bonding, no guidance or nurturing, and hugs and kisses gave when we were young.

It never occurred to me to tell anyone what was going on. Not even my twin sister would bear witness to my sexual abuse as it would undoubtedly be all my fault. Back then, there were no means of reaching out or getting help with sexual abuse, the subject considered taboo. I had no best friend or someone I could confide. There was no sex education at school, and no hotlines or helplines to help educate and encourage open and candid discussion. Even then, I had to keep the standards, stay loyal to the family, keep it private, and play the charade that all was well. I didn't dare go to Mom as I always figured it would get back to Dad, that no one would believe me, and I would get the blame. I went to school, came home, kept quiet, and didn't talk to anyone. Life went on as "normal," and I did what I was told to do. I never wanted to be in trouble; that was a really big thing for me, so I did what I thought was right, and expected of me. I didn't skip school, rebel or act out. I tried hard at school, and most of all I behaved.

Tess spent most of her time with Nina Long, her closest friend.

One night, Tess sneaked Nina inside, and like a mouse, they tiptoed up into our bedroom. Perplexed, I said to Tess, "Nina can't stay - it's almost bedtime." Tess responded in a whisper, "She's staying the night. Don't let Mom and Dad know - she's running away from home." Panic-stricken, I asked, "Where is she going to sleep?" and calmly Tess said, "We can hide her under the bed, put blankets and pillows down." Dismayed, I played along, alarmed that at any point we would get caught. An hour or so later, a gentle knock at the front door came as Nina's father had come looking for her. I cringed as Dad called Tess and me downstairs to ask if we had seen Nina or knew of her whereabouts. The porch light casts a stark, illuminating silhouette that caused his worried, pallid look to be even more pronounced. We pleaded ignorance, and the seriousness of the situation amplified my guilt of deception. Returning upstairs, I said to Nina, "Maybe you shouldn't do this, maybe you should just go home - your Dad is worried." Her hesitation visible, she said, "I can't go home now - my Dad will kill me!" The finality of her words seemed to echo our certainty that it had progressed too far, and it was now too late to back out. We all spent a sleepless night, and I lay white-knuckled as it suddenly registered, "I hope Dad doesn't choose tonight to come and get me from my bed."

I started babysitting a boy about the age of five to effectuate my desire to earn money at thirteen years old. An exuberant, likable boy, we got along well from the start. One day, innocently enough, he openly admitted to me, "My Mom and Dad run around the house naked and take pictures of themselves. I can show you if you want." With that, he was off to collect the stash of instant Polaroid pictures scattered discreetly around the house. Feeling uncomfortable with this newly acquired information, I kept quiet to avoid an awkward, embarrassing exchange of words. This further embedded my notion that everyone was involved in some degree of sexual exploitation, and it was more common than I thought. The unsettling drive home late one night cemented my uneasy feeling that his father was aware that I knew of his escapades. He did not broach the subject, but I wasn't asked to babysit again, which was answer enough.

The last babysitting extravaganza was to look after two young girls, Monica and Betty. Monica, the older of the two, was around ten, and Betty about six. A full-time summer job, Tess passed it on to me. I would babysit during the day while their parents were at work and was left to my own devices to tend to their needs. One day suggesting that I fill my day ironing their Mother's tossed aside, piled high stack of laundry, and do random chores around the house. She had enough gumption to say, "I'll pay you an extra $5.00." I didn't think I had the right to question her authority, and begrudgingly took over her duties. Another day, ever so bold, she asked, "Would you be kind enough to take Monica and Betty to the community center for the day?" I didn't want this extra responsibility, and the only lame excuse I could come up with was, "I don't know where it is." Undaunted, she said, "I'll get you the address, and give you the directions for the bus route. It will do them good to get out." I couldn't argue, and the next day we embarked on our journey. The steady transfer of buses was all-consuming as we bid our time waiting impatiently for the next bus to arrive. Waiting on the sidewalk holding Betty by the hand, I spotted the oncoming bus. A hair-raising split second is all it took for Betty to spring from my grasp in her excitement to board the bus, and straight into the path of the approaching bus. The bus driver was already coming to a stop, pumped his brakes harder, and came to a halt, inches away from hitting her. Stunned, and visibly shaken, the bus driver and I held each other's gaze as we both breathed a sigh of relief. Grabbing hold of Betty to get her out of any further harm's way, I knelt down to explain to her, "You must stay on the sidewalk - you can get hurt. From now on, do not let go of my hand." The rest of the bus trip, I grabbed her hand so tightly, in fear she might do it again. At this point, I already knew I was going to be in a whole heap of trouble. Sure enough, when I arrived the next morning, I soon learned that Monica had blurted out, "Betty almost died - the bus almost hit her!" That was all, no more details, and I had every insult thrown at me. Cursing and yelling, their Mother voiced her contempt. Without waiting or letting me explain, I had the door slammed in my face, and was told never to come back. It still haunts me to this day, not only the guilt over Betty but that I didn't have the chance to explain, to say it had been an unfortunate accident. I wanted her to realize I was responsible, not reckless as she thought. This incident hampered my willingness and motivation and brought about the end of babysitting.

Billy, now eighteen, came and went as he pleased. My parents were privy to his unruly, undisciplined ways, and decided it was the time he moves out. To Billy's surprise, my parents were waiting up for him late one night upon his return home. With dogged determination, my Mom simply stated, "I think it's time you move out." Their reasoning was, Billy had a job, and he was hardly ever home. Billy, miffed by her outright statement, stood speechless, baffled. Minutes later, he asked, "Where am I going to go?" and Mom retorted, "I'm sure you can find somewhere to stay - if not, go sleep in the park." Billy left that night with a sleeping bag in hand and ended up renting a house with a few of his friends.

My first boyfriend, Norman Russell, who I'd met at school, was an average, somewhat immature adolescent. His lack of maturity caused him to be socially awkward. His parents owned and operated a motel and were absent most of the time. With little supervision, given the freedom, and trust to look after himself. Most of my free time was spent hanging out with him at his living quarters atop the motel. The attraction, what pulled me in was I wasn't threatened by him. His lack of experience and clumsy ways were charming. He would shower me with candy and chocolates, which I thought was a romantic and alluring quality.

The preconceived notion that I would save myself for marriage was foremost, and I figured even with what Dad did, that didn't count. I wasn't promiscuous, and even though we partook in some innocent hanky-panky, I would not allow it to go further. I still had to hold on to my integrity.

Are you in the mood for amusement? An afternoon of foolery was to cut through our lowly, pedestrian existence. With nothing better to do, a bunch of us would hang out at the forested trails, a network of shortcuts running alongside our school property. I pulled Tess aside and whispered, "Pretend you are me and make out with Norman!" Laughing, I said, "Come on Tess - it'll be fun; let's see if he'll know!" Playing along, she started necking with him, and soon enough it became hot and heavy. My charade had backfired as he was oblivious to our deception. Perturbed by their show of affection, their enjoyment carried too far, I stormed over, grabbed Tess, and abruptly made her stop. Incensed by Norman's inability to know the difference, I furiously screamed out, "We were playing a trick on you. You were making out with Tess. How could you not know!?" Angered by my deception, my mockery of him, he retaliated. With no holds barred, I continued my tirade, deeply hurt, and resentful. Growing exasperated, I shouted, "You don't even know me!" and stormed off. Even Tess got a piece of my mind as I unceremoniously said, "Boy, you sure were enjoying yourself. Why didn't you stop!?" Norman's betrayal was the turning point in our relationship, and it went spiraling downhill from there on end.

The phrase, "The dark night of the soul," best exemplifies my plight. As time progressed, isolation and solitude became a much sought-after escapism. The helplessness and despair I were feeling were constant reminders that I had no one to turn to and was completely alone. I would immerse myself in activities that required no thought, just mindless action. To channel my pent-up energy, I went bike riding. The freedom to go the distance, however far, on my terms. The exhilaration as the cool breeze against my face heightened the rush as I sped down the quiet streets shrouded in darkness. Other than that, I enjoyed the park, and at the creek would sit mesmerized by the flow and the relaxing sound of the gurgling water. I would draw; it seemed I had a natural talent, and nature itself was my canvas. I took up tennis, learning against the backboard by myself, and the repetitive "thwonk" of the tennis ball was calming. Poetry became my outlet, and I immersed myself in music. I would sing along to John Denver, the Eagles, and the Beach Boys, to name a few. My favorite songs, "Leaving on a Jet Plane" by John Denver, "House of the Rising Sun" by the Animals, and "Down on the Corner" by Creedence Clearwater Revival. I would treasure solitude; this was my escape, and I didn't have to be at home.

I had a love for animals. We had no short supply of puppies as Tippy, our Maltipoo, wasn't spayed, and continuously had a litter of puppies running around the house. One of her puppies she pushed away shortly after giving birth and would not let her suckle. I took a toy baby bottle and tried to nurse it back to health. Spending hours, holding and nurturing this puppy, I was hoping she would come around. She died during the night, and I can only guess that there had to have been something wrong inside.

Tippy followed us to school one day without us knowing. She stayed behind and was struck by a car as she tried to cross the street. Left for dead, no one stopped. My Dad, unbeknownst to us, found her lifeless body lying on the side of the road. It wasn't until we came home from school we were told. Her death affected all of us and, from then on, we never got another dog.

Taking notice of nature, I would spot the obscure, slithering garter snake. Hear the cheery song of the Orange-breasted American Robin. Watch the blue jay busily hiding the nuts for a later day, like the squirrels. Catch the flying grasshopper jump, and even discern the minuscule, marching procession of the common ants. My excitement at pointing out a garter snake dashed when my Dad would grab it and proceed to smash it against a tree. Another time, baby birds nestled in the eaves of our bedroom attic knocked to the ground, and my Dad's only comment was to say, "Birds are a nuisance; they make a mess." I decided from that point on to stop telling him what I saw.

I had always tried to do well in school and, never receiving help at home with homework, managed to keep my grades up by myself. I did ask my parents for help once, but both were unable to grasp or figure out the homework assignment, so I stopped asking.

When report cards issued, it was only to get my parents' signature. No praise was forthcoming at home, and the only form of acknowledgment came if you didn't do well, and then you heard about it. Any little bit of recognition I received was by a few select teachers, which I gladly accepted.

For the most part, drawn to the "outcasts," - teachers and students alike. One older teacher taught algebra, and she wasn't a favorite among the students. She reeked of liquor, and you knew she had a drinking problem; but to me, she was kind and helpful. I excelled in Algebra, typing, shorthand, and business machines, all of which she taught. It was nice to have someone recognize my work and ability and take notice with just a few words of encouragement.

I'll never forget the day I went to school, and during the middle of the class started feeling quite nauseated. Projects due, the students were milled about the teacher's desk. Squeamishly, I approached the teacher, and unable to talk repeatedly tapped him on the shoulder to get his attention. I was getting ignored, but I have to say I wasn't ignored for long as I spewed forth vomit all over his desk. The kids quickly scattered in disgust and, the teacher agitated and revolted by my untimely act, asked, "Why couldn't you throw up in the garbage can or go to the bathroom?" My response, "I tried to get your attention to ask permission to go to the bathroom." He retorted, "Next time just go!" Never before had I been so embarrassed!

Tess and I didn't hang out together at school. She went her way, and I went mine. I remember on one occasion walking down the hallway, and a heavy, overbearing girl stormed towards me. Her actions were loud and clear as she was bent on an all-out brawl. Her belligerence at the very sight of me ushered forth a battery of verbal insults. Dumbfounded, I firmly stood as I was clueless as to who this crazed person was. Indignant at my unmoving, implausible reaction, she said, "Come on Tess - what's the matter, you too afraid to fight?" I answered matter-of-factly, "I'm not Tess," and she thought I was lying to avoid a fight. I again said, "I'm not Tess; I'm Anna, Tess is my twin sister." Her expression was one of utter amazement and, with questionable doubt, she taunted me by saying, "You'd better be telling me the truth or else I'll come and find you!" As an afterthought, she said, "Tell Tess I'm looking for her," and all I could say was, "Okay, what's your name?"

Smoking marijuana was a means of fitting in, wanting to be accepted as part of the crowd. Coupled with peer pressure, it can be a deadly mixture. The first time I used marijuana was on a Saturday night at a local hang-out park. Tess was meeting up with her friends and insisted I come along. Dusk precipitated the preparation, and joints were getting rolled. All of us gathered in a circle, and the joint circulated. As my turn came, someone said, "Here, take a toke." I took a puff and instantaneously started to cough. Handing it back, I said, "I don't want anymore," hurt that Tess hadn't been honest about her true intentions to meet up with friends to get high. The mood was a helter-skelter of boisterous, unrestrained flight as everyone now high ran around in silly, careless abandonment. I became increasingly uncomfortable with the atmosphere and pretended to play along as I did not want to stick out like a sore thumb.

Another time, Tess would offer me a drink. We were in the bushes beside the school one morning and pulling out a paper bag tucked away in her jacket, she reached in and withdrew a flask of liquor. Not contrite in the least, she said, "Here, have a drink" as she offered up the flask. Astonished, I looked at her and asked, "Where did you get it?" and she replied, "It's Dad's; I sneaked it out of the house." Shocked by her admission and, wanting no part of getting drunk, I refused. I couldn't believe she could even think of having a drink first thing in the morning right before school. I kept her company until the bell rang, and then I turned to go, waiting for her to come. She said, "I'm not going; I'm skipping school today. I'm meeting up with Nina - don't tell Mom." It was at this moment I knew she was intent on doing her thing, her way, and headed in the direction she wanted to take. The next day, I thought to myself maybe Tess is right, and I too snuck out my stash of Dad's liquor. I left early for school and returned to the same spot. Obscuring myself from sight, I took a little sip thinking, "Okay, if Tess can do it, so can I." Well, it didn't work, it wasn't me, and I poured the rest out. It wasn't long before Dad wised up to his watered-down bottles of liquor, and the shit hit the fan.

It always seemed I had a basic instinct of knowing the right from the wrong and, even though I was a follower, I never had the inclination to get involved in drugs, drinking, stealing or lying. I only started smoking at sixteen to fit in as peer pressure got the upper hand. I guess you could call me a "Goody Two-Shoes," a term I detest; enough so, that it would solidify the fact I didn't fit in anywhere: not with the popular crowd, the troublemakers or the brainy kids called the "nerds."

Tess, Nina, and I went to the mall one afternoon, and I was encouraged to shoplift. They said, "The jewelry hanging from the display racks is easy to steal. Pretend you are browsing, and then casually tuck it into your hand." Trying, I succeeded in placing it in my hand, but then my moral instincts kicked in, and I had no option other than to place it back on the rack.

Tess's clandestine ways would prove to be outlandish and foolish. This time, I tagged along to a house party that she and Nina were invited. The first stop was to the liquor store and, being underage, Tess convinced a stranger to buy it for her. We arrived with the liquor in hand to find Nina already partying with three disreputable looking men. A dingy, rundown house, it was sparse of furnishings. An uneasiness came over me when I realized these men were much older; not even close to our age. I soon learned that Tess and Nina had a brief encounter with them at some other party and did not know the first thing about them. About an hour or so in, I couldn't shake the feeling of dread as my gut told me they were up to no good. Their intentions were to get us drunk, and into bed. An overwhelming sense of foreboding came over me, so much so, I was scared. I whispered to Tess, "I think we should leave; I don't have a good feeling about this. Come on, let's go now!" The only time I was able to convince Tess to listen to me.

Tess and I were opposites and thus went in completely different directions. Tess was defiant and rebellious, whereas I was submissive and compliant. Tess had a tendency of looking out for herself, and she would not bow down to anyone. I admired that about Tess; she wasn't afraid what anyone thought, but it sure got her into a whole heap of trouble. I, on the other hand, had to keep control, not get into any trouble and was steadfast in looking for approval. That was the motivator - I couldn't lose control, and I was looking for acceptance instead.

One day after we had all got home from school, we were playing out in the yard. Dad was still at work, and my Mom was in the kitchen preparing supper. Melanie came up to me and whispered, "Can you come with me? I want to show you something." Glancing nervously around, she said, "Be very quiet; I don't want Mom to hear," and we made our way silently into the house through the basement door. She took me to the workshop, reached up to the window sill, and pulled out a canister concealed in the back. Hesitantly, she emptied out the contents and showed me the all-so-familiar pornographic cards. I was in a panic as I thought, "Oh no, she knows about me!" I mustered up all my courage to pretend it was nothing and tried to be nonchalant, but all the while I was trembling inside. I stymied any chances of communication as I thought, "She knows about me! - she found the cards by accident, she is going to tell, and it will be all my fault." I was in a rush to leave, anxious to forget it ever happened. Melanie had come to me in confidence, and that was my mistake - I didn't know.

My Dad

The lessons I was taught by my Dad – I wish I had seen,
For only bitterness and pity followed, for what could have been.
He came into my life when I was two;
And that was when I was first confused -
For I did not know why my name had changed,
to one that I could not spell or gauge.
The early years were good, I must say,
for he had become the father, I don't know today.
The moments I remember – picnics in the park,
and even though we were poor, presents from the start.
He'd play his guitar and sing along,
to a tape recording of a Johnny Cash song.
He had become our provider, no easy feat,
considering there were five children he had to keep.
And when I turned twelve, my life would change -
You see, even then I was naive.

Came the secret I could never tell,
my father sexually abused me – living in hell.
And if I told, I knew it would be,
all my fault – for sure to be.
Deep inside, I knew it was wrong,
but where could I turn? I had to be strong.
Oh, the lessons I learned... that I was getting taught,
my childhood taken and all but forgot.
I hated the world; I did not speak,
and kept the secret way down deep.
For years, this went on; tension was high,
I avoided my Dad, for it had to stop or die.
To this day, I find it hard to trust -
For now, earned, and that's a must.
Though I have learned to forgive – it's sad
for I'm still asking, "Why did you do it, Dad?"

Seven

In the hubbub of putting groceries away one night, it finally dawned on Mom that Melanie was nowhere in sight. Mom called out to her and, not getting any answer, told us, "Go find Melanie; she's got to be here somewhere." We searched the house but couldn't find her. Wondering where else she could be, I thought, "Maybe she's in the basement." It didn't make any sense why she would go down to the basement, but I thought I'd better go check. As I set foot in the basement, I glanced around for any signs of Melanie. Hearing a muted sound coming from the corner of the room, I headed over in that direction. Puzzled, I perked my ears to see if I could find the source of the noise. The muffled sound was coming from inside the wall and, looking down noticed the hook unlatched to the built-in storage compartment. My curiosity peaked, I reached down to open the door, and to my shock, there was Melanie crouched with her knees tucked up to her chest in this cramped, 50 cm x 50 cm confined space. Cuddling herself in a little ball, she rocked back and forth giving no indication of my presence. Mystified and baffled, I said, "Melanie, what are you doing in there? Come out - Mom's looking for you!" Expressionless, and with no answer, she crawled out and headed upstairs.

Another time, we were playing downstairs in the basement, and Melanie did the most incredulous thing. She raced, round and around the pool table in a frenzied bound. She circled the pool table with such an intensity my head started to spin just by watching her. Giving no signs of slowing down or stopping, I called out, "What are you doing

Melanie?" She gave no reaction other than a crazed look and, in hysterics, she persisted in her peculiar behavior. Exasperated, I just assumed she was acting silly, and I walked away.

One night, while sitting at the kitchen table doing my homework, an unexpected knock came at the back door. Now dark outside, it was impossible to see the two policemen at our door with Tess, Melanie, and Helen in tow. The police escorting them in said, "Your kids were caught breaking into Douglas Road School along with a couple of their friends." I sat flabbergasted as the police informed my parents of the break-in, the incurred damages, and the vandalism to the school. A pivotal moment as bedlam was to follow.

There was a lot of friction in our house, and the tension was so thick you could cut it with a knife. Tess was getting into a whole lot of trouble at school, which instigated a shouting match as my Mom and Dad confronted Tess about her truancy. Tess, more defiant than ever, wouldn't back down, which infuriated Dad, and it turned physical. I sat at the kitchen table wishing I could be anywhere other than where I was. I didn't dare interfere, and my only thought was for Tess to stop. Just stop Tess, then you won't be in trouble. My Dad, thrown into a fit of rage by Tess's defiance, lashed out and slapped Tess so hard it sent her reeling across the floor. Like a wounded animal, Tess's immediate fight or flight response kicked in, and she turned to run. Storming out the back door, she bellowed her verbal assault in protest and retreated. My Mom, siding with my Dad, did nothing to stop the skirmish. Running outside after Tess, I found her on the back porch pacing back and forth in agitation, her breathing labored, and clenching her fists. Her emotions of hurt, frustration, and anger were palpable as she stated, "I'm outta here! Can you get my glasses for me? He knocked them off." Back inside, I scouted the entire floor to find Tess's glasses. Spotting them, I bent down and picked up the slightly warped, bent frames. My Mom, still agitated and worked up, asked sternly, "What are you doing?" Afraid of her reprisal, and not wanting to be in trouble myself, I whispered, "I'm getting Tess's glasses." She retorted, "Tell Tess to get back inside." I nodded, and quietly headed back out the door.

Concerned for Tess's welfare, I asked her what she was going to do. She said, "I'm not going back inside. I'll stay at Nina's tonight." Feeling ill at ease, I sat indecisive and unsure of what to do. The situation was beyond resolving, and I felt helpless. Tess, growing fearful that Dad would soon be out, said, "I'd better go." I went back inside and relayed the message to Mom that Tess wasn't coming back tonight, and quickly left to go to bed.

The phrase, "Three strikes and you're out," certainly applied to our now disastrous, wretched home life; talk about a prison sentence, there was no escaping the confines of our punishment.

My Mom, desperate and, not knowing where else to turn, thought a counselor might be able to help. I had to laugh as our entire family sat pathetically in the counselor's office and didn't utter a word. Even the prompting by the counselor wasn't enough for us to open up; it may have helped if we had private one-on-one sessions, but with my Mom and Dad in the room, nothing was getting discussed. The counselor, as a last-ditch effort asked, "Is there anything you want to talk about?" After a long, awkward silence, I finally said, "Our dog died; she got hit by a car, and we're all upset."

At a loss, my Mom turned to spiritual inspiration and guidance since counseling hadn't worked. Deciding it was about time she attends Church service, she propositioned all of us to come, and I was the only one up for it. My Dad, an Atheist, did not agree with my Mom's Roman Catholic upbringing and had no reverence for religion or the beliefs of the Church. Dad's cynicism weighed heavily on our childhood as, from the start, he would not tolerate any practices or worship to do with the Church. Sunday mass at the Holy Rosary Cathedral in downtown Vancouver proved to be a new experience for me as I had never stepped foot inside a church. The church service was foreign to me, left me anxious and, to mollify my uneasiness, I followed my Mom's lead. At the end of the service, while the priest shook hands with my Mom and thanked her for attending, she presumptuously voiced her concerns about our discontented family life. The priest, a very amicable, outgoing individual, offered his services to come to our house. Within the week, he was sitting at our kitchen table having a cup of coffee, and a good-natured talk with Dad! My Dad, unknowingly, had been put on the spot, and my Mom was purposely absent. The meeting scheduled behind my Dad's back and all my Mom's valiant efforts were defeated as Dad was adamant that he would not entertain this deceit again.

Taking a trip to Disneyland in Anaheim, California, would be the first vacation our family ever had. It's funny how certain memories you retain more than others. Our tires slashed as we spent the night in a seedy motel room along the way, and the next morning waking up to find every tire completely flat. Stopping at a tourist attraction, my Mom wanted to tour a small, quaint historic Mexican church nestled in the outskirts. Proceeding down the aisle between the pews of this tiny church, my Dad quite brazenly showed his disapproval and contempt of God by making snide remarks. Thinking himself quite funny and witty, he had the audacity to laugh at his sarcasm and slurs. His voice loud, cut through with little regard and disrupted the quiet serenity of this sanctuary. Ashamed by his actions, I nervously giggled and was grateful that no other tourists or staff were within earshot; this was the one and the only vacation we spent together as a family other than Billy, who had to work. My Dad's birthday coincided with our vacation, and as a gesture of kindness, I handed him a $100 bill, a gift I'd saved up from babysitting. I honestly thought I could change things, his behavior, and stop the sexual abuse. Unfortunately, our lives went back to how it was before, and the vacation gave us only a break, a lapse in our routine.

Then came the night police knocked on our door. Melanie had attempted suicide by trying to jump off the Lougheed Highway overpass on Highway 1. Someone driving by noticed Melanie hanging off the rail, and promptly called the police. A policeman managed to talk her down after a two-hour standoff. Melanie was admitted to the Burnaby Mental Health Unit that night; it was April 20, 1978.

Even then, Melanie still gave no indication of what was wrong. I visited Melanie one afternoon with Mom, and a sense of desolation enveloped the dreary white-washed private room. Melanie seemed lost, out of sorts, and not herself. She only spoke when spoken to and, even then, her answers were short and brief. Too cheery, a front, she kept her true feelings and inner turmoil hidden. Visiting hours over, my Mom went to talk to the on-duty nurse to ask about the medications Melanie was on, how she was coping, and if there was any change or improvement. She said, "I'm worried; Melanie won't talk to me." The nurse replied, "She's doing good; she's taking an interest, and participating in the group sessions." After a lengthy discussion about Melanie's progress, the nurse turned and pointed at me, and jokingly remarked, "I think it's her you need to worry about." I looked at her, stunned, and became uncomfortable with the attention she had drawn to me. My Mom oblivious, shrugged it off, unaware at how very close the nurse had come to sense that something wasn't quite right.

I would visit Melanie in the ward and go to school by myself. On the first occasion, Melanie led me down the somber, eerily quiet hallway to a large room used for group therapy sessions. The room filled with therapy equipment and in one corner a collection of soft foam bats and balls. Pointing to the bats, I asked Melanie, "What are those for?" and she picked up a bat explaining, "We take the bats, and bash each other like this. It's supposed to be a game to release our frustrations and anger - do you wanna try?" I replied, "No, not really." Back in her room, Melanie went to her bedside dresser drawer and pulled out a couple of craft items she had made - one being a handcrafted leather wallet, and the other a clay sculpture. The sculpture a frightening portrayal of a hideous monster had protruding horns on top of its head, the elongated claws were curved and sharp, and the fangs descended from its grimacing snarl. We sat on the bed and Melanie, even though obliging on the surface, masked her problems.

The second and final time I went to visit Melanie, she was outside sitting motionless on the swing. She was due to get discharged in a day or so, only a week and a half into her stay. Her placid, stoic composure was disquieting. Going up and saying hi, I found her uncommunicative, expressionless, and unresponsive. With a blank, empty stare and, void of emotion, she sat listlessly. "Melanie," I asked, "What's wrong?" In a monotone voice, she replied, "I've made up my mind; I've decided what to do." I asked, "What have you decided to do?" I waited, but she would not answer, and just sat forlornly with an empty stare.

The day she was released on April 30, 1978, she would once again return to the same overpass. At 10:15 p.m., she jumped from the overpass and was certified dead at Burnaby Hospital at 10:30 p.m. I did not find out until I got home from work. As I made my way up the back steps, I peered in the kitchen window and was surprised to see Aunt Sue and Uncle Barry were over. From what I could see, everyone was standing around in the kitchen. A nagging feeling crept in, and surprise turned to dread as the scene unfolded in front of me. A thick cloud hung over the room as the sounds of sobbing, and grief-stricken screams filled the air. Looking over, I saw Mom crying in hysterics, and any efforts my Dad made to console her were pushed away. Desperately, I searched the mournful, dire faces looking for an explanation. I stood frozen at the door for what seemed an eternity until Uncle Barry came over to me. The harsh realization, sinking in as he told me, "Melanie's died - she jumped off the bridge. Tess and Julie tried to talk her down, but it was no use." The memory of Melanie's words that fateful day drifted back, and I shuddered at her words, an omen. She made up her mind, and this time there would be no talking her out of it. I couldn't believe I had just been on the bus heading home and, without even knowing, had driven right over the spot where Melanie had taken her life on the pavement below, Lougheed Highway. I was sick to my stomach. Why did no one call me or come and get me from work? How could they make me wait, and not tell me? I was deeply hurt and felt betrayed.

In total disbelief and not wanting to believe what I was hearing, I bolted and bounded out the back door frantic to get to the bridge. The rain had lightened somewhat, but a thick veil of dark clouds still blanketed the evening sky. In the eerily quiet, somber night, I ran as if possessed, intent on getting to the overpass. I was in complete denial, lost all judgment, and all I knew was I had to get there and be with Melanie. Uncle Barry ran after me, and grabbing hold of me said, "Stop, you can't do this." Angry, I screamed, "Let me go - I have to be with

Melanie!" and twisted desperately, trying to break his hold. Agonizingly, I cried out in pain, "How could Melanie die!?" I broke down, collapsing, empty inside. I withered into my inner sanctum, lost, and completely alone. Melanie wasn't supposed to die.

We all grieved alone, quite literally on our own. There was no comfort, no solace, and everyone in a grief-stricken state of mind. Before the funeral, I went with Mom to the private viewing room, so that she wouldn't be alone. Standing in front of the casket, my Mom touched Melanie's perfectly crisscrossed positioned hands as if to comfort her and, with desperation in her voice, whispered, "Oh my God, she's so cold." She then gently reached up to rectify the lopsided crucifix, a necklace my Mom asked the funeral home to place around Melanie's neck. I stood watching in silence as Mom caressed Melanie's hair, and commented on how you couldn't tell (couldn't see the damage to her skull), then said, "It looks just like Melanie's sleeping." In the final moment, my Mom bent down to gently kiss Melanie one last time. Staring down at Melanie's body, I froze, terrified that at any minute she would open her eyes. To this day, when I go to a funeral, I cannot view the person who died.

Thinking back, I was so naive and never believed Melanie would take her life. I thought, "She's getting help - they'll help her; she'll be okay." I should have seen the signs, obvious now, but I didn't know, and I was guilt-ridden. I would have nightmares of Melanie chasing after me, wielding an ax, bent on seeking revenge. Her malevolent, crazed look intensified, transforming into a zombie in her pursuit to kill me. The black cloud of fear grew as I ran down the darkened, shadowy twists of corridors to escape her rage. The dank odor of death permeated the air, choking me, and my legs felt heavy and weighed me down. A slow-motion horror movie, as each nook and cranny I turned to go into to hide, was a futile endeavor. At every step, Melanie was behind me unyieldingly swinging the ax, ready to strike - the startling jolt as I awoke, succumbing to the final blow. Beads of perspiration and my shallow breathing were testaments to the sheer terror and misery I felt.

Up to this point, no one knew what was wrong with Melanie -

why she had attempted, and then committed suicide. My Mom speculated she had got in with a bad crowd and influenced into doing drugs. The abuse was still a secret, and no one knew.

After the funeral, I started hanging out with Ricky, Melanie's last boyfriend. Ricky was older than Melanie, more my age, and lived at home with his divorced father. By chance, we ran into each other one day and both of us succumbing to grief leaned on each other for emotional support. Ricky opened up and professed his mental anguish as he too felt responsible for Melanie's death. He confessed, "Melanie broke up with me because she thought she was pregnant. I told Melanie that I would look after her, we could get married, and it would be okay. I told her we could go to your parents and tell them. My Dad may not approve, but he will understand." He went on to say, "Melanie resisted my ideas, was angry over my answers, and we quarreled. She left stating our relationship was over and didn't want to see me again." Ricky didn't see Melanie after that and, even though he tried to reach out, Melanie would not speak to him. I kept this to myself, wondering if this was why Melanie had finally snapped. Had she been pregnant and, if so, was it enough to make her go off the deep end?

For many years after, the questions remained, "Was Melanie abused? Was she pregnant?" If Melanie thought she was pregnant, she must have felt trapped in a situation that was hard to imagine, let alone understand. If abused, the mere thought of not knowing if Dad was the father was a grim possibility, and a nightmare at only 14 years old. The black hole of depression had to have been all-consuming, and she must have been desperate enough to think she had no way out.

There was no proof, no way of finding out the truth, and it was a puzzle, to which I would never have the answer. Much later, my Mom told me Dad had a vasectomy, but still, the question remained, "Was Melanie abused?" I thought I was the only one.

There was an inquest to determine if anything could have been done to prevent Melanie's suicide, and recommendations were made for the Burnaby Mental Health Unit to make changes to their policies. Pamela Martin, of BCTV News, came to our house and interviewed my Mom. The next day, Melanie had made the evening news.

It was at this point at the inquest I found out Dad was my stepfather. I thought, "That would explain why we don't all look the same." Billy, born of Italian descent, had a slim physique, was shorter in stature, olive skinned, and had brown hair and eyes. Helen, being Ukrainian, was also slim and short, but had blonde hair and blue eyes. Melanie, with dirty blonde hair and brown eyes, was petite, and closer in appearance to Helen. I was to learn that she was not my stepsister, but Peter was her biological father as well. The secrets kept coming as I found out my Mom and Dad weren't married right away. It wasn't until we lived on Sprott Street, they secretly went out one night and eloped.

I remember that night as it deviated from the typical routine and, besides, my Mom and Dad rarely went out. My Mom said, "We're going out for the night; we'll be home in the morning," and left Billy in charge. That was the night Billy abandoned all responsibility and, without my parents' consent, threw a wild, no-holds-barred party. With the liquor flowing and the steady drone of the music blaring, the jam-packed crowd spilling into the backyard into the wee hours of the morning. Caught up in the excitement, the vigorous energy, we were too enthralled and wired up to sleep. Early the next morning, my parents arrived home to a yard and basement littered with the aftereffects of the all-night party, and a visit by Norm Russett, our neighbor, to complain and inform our parents of the previous night's escapade.

One night not long after Melanie died, my Mom, in a solemn and glum mood, said softly, "It's bedtime; go upstairs, and go to bed." We didn't make a fuss, not in the state she was in, and obliged. Tess and Helen had fallen asleep, but I restlessly laid awake. The sounds of my Mom and Dad arguing filtered up in the stillness of the late night. I was straining to hear; their muted voices were indiscernible. All of a sudden, it went quiet, too quiet, which was unnerving and unsettling. I crept out of bed and tiptoed down the stairs. Peering around the corner, I noticed Dad standing in the kitchen, but my Mom was nowhere in sight. I got up enough nerve, knowing I wasn't supposed to be up, and stealthily made my way into the kitchen. Dad, standing at the counter nursing a drink, was distant, lost in thought. Guardedly, I asked, "Dad, where's Mom?" His tone noncommittal, he muttered, "She's out back," and with a wave of dismissal, refilled his drink.

With a sense of foreboding I shuddered, and in my pajamas, I searched the backyard for any clues or signs of movement or disturbance. My eyes not yet adjusted to the dark, I stumbled upon Mom by chance by almost tripping over her sprawled out body lying in the coolness of the dewy grass. Finding her lethargic, but not unconscious, I knelt down to ask her what she was doing. Her response muddled, and her expression clouded, she lapsed once more into a lethargic state. Grabbing her shoulders, I shook her fervently to make her snap out of it. Unresponsive, a slight mumble was her only answer. Racing back to the house, I screamed at Dad, "Come get Mom; there's something wrong - she won't get up!" He carried, and half dragged, her listless body back to the house as he cursed under his breath all the while. Leaning her up against the kitchen countertop, he as calm as a cucumber, slapped her several times across the face to wake her up. By this point, Tess and Helen alerted by the commotion, woke up, and rushed down to the kitchen. We all yelled for him to stop, but my Dad wasn't in any mood to explain his actions and shouted, "Come hold her up - I have to make coffee." Attempting to make her drink coffee failed, and he tried shoving the black, steaming hot coffee down her throat. Concern turned to panic as I was afraid the boiling coffee had scalded her. My heart broke at the sight of my Mom's beleaguered state as I inspected her coffee-soaked torso for signs of burns. My Mom still comatose and, with my Dad's efforts not working, my Dad conceded, and phoned for an ambulance. Rushed to Burnaby Hospital, they said she had taken an overdose of pills, and proceeded to pump her stomach out. She insisted she did not need the help of a psychiatrist and admitted she had mistakenly mixed her drinking with pills. Life was not the same after Melanie died, and still, no one knew why Melanie died.

Melanie

There were so many signs we did not see
Remembering the time when I searched high and low,
she had been hiding in a cubbyhole.
I opened the closet, and there I found,
Melanie huddled in the corner – not a sound.
She would not speak, she would not say,
what anguish she was keeping buried 'way.
And then the time she raced 'round and 'round,
the pool table, in a frenzied bound.
A peculiar smile and hysterical laughter,
I would ask her, "What's the matter?"
The last time I would hear her talk,
Was when she told me what she thought -
A weight lifted from her shoulders she knew,
for she had decided what to do.
Suicide it seemed was her only way,
and she jumped to her death from a bridge one day.
Only fourteen, she could not have foreseen,
that time alone would heal all wounds not seen.

Eight

When Tess and I turned sixteen, Dad took us to a used car dealership in Burnaby. He said, "I'll buy you both a car, but you'll have to make the payments." Browsing through the selection of the cheapest cars available on the lot, I chose a 1964 Pontiac Parisienne, and my Dad co-signed the loan. I was over the moon as Tess got her car, and I got mine. It was exhilarating to have my car, and now I had the freedom and luxury of driving.

The brutality of the situation as I thought I had escaped my predicament. In between work and school, I was unaware of the crisis brewing at home. One afternoon while returning home from school, my Mom summoned Tess and me together. Not wasting any time, she said, "I've rented an apartment for you both. Go pack your things, and I'll drive you there." She did not allude to my queries, and simply stated, "Hurry up; I want to go before Dad gets home." There was no discussion as we were getting treated perfunctorily, and at sixteen years old, Tess, and I were on our own. I didn't question it and just assumed she finally had enough of the fighting, the conflict at home. The sexual abuse was still a secret; no one knew. Talk about being thrown from the frying pan into the fire, and I was at a loss. The apartment, a furnished one-bedroom suite on Franklin Street in Burnaby, was adequate, but it bore the remnants of a well-worn pair of shoes. Tess got the bedroom, and I slept on the couch. My Mom said, "I've paid the first month's rent, and I'll buy you groceries to get you going." As if nothing else could go wrong, I was without a car. Dad was adamant about keeping the cars as Tess wasn't making her payments. He was too afraid he would get stuck paying both our loans. I wasn't pleased as I had always kept my side of the bargain and paid my loan, but he would not return my keys. Left out in the cold, I made the necessary adjustments to my life.

My Mom, working at the TD Bank Data Centre, was able to get me hired on when I was 15 years old after putting in a good word. I had to lie about my age and say I didn't have a social insurance number (which wasn't a lie) since the job age requirement was 16 and over. While starting in the mail room, my duties were to sort the incoming/outgoing mail from the various branches. One night, with work being rather slack, I busied myself "spring cleaning." I tackled the chore of organizing the accumulation of long forgotten, tossed mailbags thrown in a heap into the storage bins. I was awe-struck as one of the bags I opened was full of money, and the stack of bills bound with bank wrappers. I turned it over to the Supervisor, and she was as shocked as I was. Unable to trace where the money originated from, I thought, at the very least, I would get a reward, but instead, I only received a thank you. I could have kicked myself as the temptation to keep the money was strong, but I wasn't one to steal. Oh well, my good deed now was done. I worked hard and got promoted four times. I didn't work the same shift as my Mom, but we would run into each other when her shift ended. My routine now was to bus it to school, and then go straight off to work. Working the evening shift, I would catch the bus, and get home around 1:00 a.m.

One typical night, I got off at the nearest bus stop and started walking the remaining way home. At this late hour, the streets were subdued, quiet, and the traffic was sparse. Minding my own business, and concentrating only on getting home, I didn't notice a car slowing down. Pulling over to the side of the road, a guy, in his late twenties or early thirties, casually yelled out his window, "Hi, where are you going?" Glancing over, and taken aback, I replied, "I'm going home." Keeping the conversation going, he asked in a friendly manner, "Do you want to go to a party?" and I politely responded, "No." Being persistent, he said,

"Okay, well here's my number; give me a call. Why don't you let me drive you home then?" I said, "No thank you, I'm almost there," and I diligently kept walking. Unwavering in his approach, he slowly drove his car in reverse to stay beside me. Persevering, with his puppy-dog eyes he pleaded, "Come on, let me drive you home." Out of patience, I finally conceded and got in his car. I thought, "What's the harm? I'll just let him drive me home." Well, it goes without saying, it was the stupidest decision I'd ever made! Giving him directions, I was dismayed, and my nerves were on edge when he drove to an isolated, dead-end street. It snowballed from there when he stopped, turned off his car, and proceeded to pull his penis from his pants. My street savvy kicked in when faced with a dire predicament, and I kept my wits about me. The only way out of this mess was to play it cool, remain calm, and composed. I could not let him see that I was scared, and I had to keep control. He was happy enough to get a hand job, nothing more, and with a slight inkling of remorse, he proceeded to start his car. Acting as if nothing was wrong, like before I repeated directions to my house. Not telling him exactly where I lived, I asked him to drop me off in the lane. Far enough away from my apartment, and yet close enough if I had to, I could run. Stepping out of his car, I said in a feigned, cheery voice, "Thanks for the ride; I'll give you a call." I didn't move until I could see he was well out of sight. Shaking uncontrollably, I entered my apartment, praying he wasn't going to turn around and head back my way. Tess wasn't home, and I was alone. Terrified, I crouched down on the couch peering through the curtains and didn't dare turn the lights on. I stayed awake all night, too afraid he was coming back. I said to myself over and over, "Stupid, how could you get in the car? I would never again be so trusting or vulnerable.

Tess while working at McDonald's on Granville Street in downtown Vancouver, managed to get me a job there. Friday nights and weekends, we both worked the graveyard shift cleaning the restaurant after closing. We made it our practice to hand out the food left over from the day to the homeless people teeming about outside. It came to an end as word got out, and we were instructed by management to throw it in the garbage instead for security reasons. The homeless, a collection of derelicts down and out on their luck, were the undesired, and many were dealing with addiction and mental health issues. They were the night-time regulars and locals we came to know on sight and the ones who owned the streets at night; this was their domain, and they willingly accepted us in part. The buses weren't running when we got off work so Tess and I would walk home. Our journey began as we made our way through the diverse cultural sections of downtown Vancouver, traversing the deserted, cobblestone streets of Gastown, through the seedy sections of Hastings Street, and ending up at the Joyce Loop Bus Station in time to take the bus the rest of the way home. The police, assuming we were up to no good, routinely stopped us, and wanted to know what we were doing out in the early morning hours. One night, on the spur of the moment, and for a change of routine, I decided to walk all the way home. Up for a challenge, and with Tess not working that night, I wanted to see how long it would take me; what started off as an adventure, turned into a grueling workout as exhaustion set within. The hours were passing, and, on my last legs, I gazed longingly over my left shoulder at an approaching bus. Determined I thought, "Nope, I'm gonna finish this." It took me four hours or so, but I painstakingly made it home. Looking back, Tess and I had spunk - resilient at only 14 years old; we were gutsy beyond our years. Susceptible to the hidden dangers, I was astounded that nothing bad ever happened to us but, the way I saw it, the danger already existed - and it was waiting for me at home.

Headline News
"All Hands on Deck, The Storm is About to Hit!"

We need to batten down the hatches; stormy weather is imminent, and we need to prepare for tough times ahead. I learned that I wasn't the only one sexually abused, and our lives would spiral, topsy-turvy - the momentum would send our family reeling out of control.

I rarely heard from Mom, so it was quite a surprise when right out of the blue, she phoned and asked if I would come with her. Being quite elusive she said, "I'll explain later." She picked me up, and I could tell she was frazzled and upset. With difficulty, and with her voice quivering, she made several attempts at discussion but stopped. Articulating her thoughts momentarily, she finally managed to blurt out, "Did you know what Dad was doing?" My stomach was churning, and in knots, I did not own up or give any inclination of being sexually abused. I played dumb, and after a brief interlude of silence I said, "No, I didn't know." Just as simple as that - my answer was brief, and to the point. In a state of shock and distress, her driving was erratic, and she was barely able to keep the car on the road. Her thoughts marked only by an intense burning need to comprehend and absorb her predicament, she continued her rampage, saying, "I'm going to confront Dad; I need you to look after Helen until I do." It didn't occur to her to ask, "Are you getting abused?" I guess her revelation and shock at one were enough. Besides, she probably thought I would have said. In her despair, she cried, "God, I hope he didn't touch Melanie - I have to find out." Squirming, I kept silent and did not tell. It was still deeply ingrained that it was all my fault, and I would get the blame. Helen came to stay with Tess and me that afternoon and, that evening, the storm hit as the confrontation had begun.

Inundated with accusations, my Dad denied everything, said it was all a lie, and nothing happened. Once he realized that Mom knew facts, he sheepishly admitted only to what he had to. My Mom kept up her assault, wanting to know about Melanie if he had ever touched her. He would deny this as there was certainly no proof and no way of finding out. He let it slip by mistake, thinking Mom knew about me as well. Caught, and this time he had tripped himself up letting the cat out of the bag. In a blind fury, my Mom burst forth and pummeled him with her fists. In total disbelief, she could not fathom how this could have happened, and it was beyond her comprehension how he could have got away with it all this time without her knowing. She phoned later that night telling us she had left Dad, needed to make arrangements, and warned us to be on the lookout for Dad as he might retaliate.

I never discussed the details of my abuse - not even with my Mom. Even after Dad let it slip, all anyone knew was, "Yeah, it happened." My Mom took Helen, left my Dad, and moved into an apartment. No one is asking what exactly happened, how I was coping or if I needed help. A short time later, to my horror, I found out she took him back! My Dad was a very good liar, had the gift of gab, and could talk himself out of any situation. He had convinced my Mom to take him back. My voice didn't count, and I felt as if I was thrown to the wayside, once again. Unbelievable how one person can have such an impact, change the lives and outcomes of those around.

They moved into an apartment building in New Westminster and became the building property managers. If I wanted to keep a relationship with Mom, I had no choice but to accept the situation. My Mom's actions had determined the outcome and, unbeknownst to me, she played it down. Maybe it was her way of dealing with it, preferring to turn a blind eye - or maybe, it was just too much for her to absorb; I don't know. What I do know, she put my Dad first, and he won out. She was unwilling to support herself and Helen and be alone.

I didn't know any better - call it being naïve or call it whatever you like. I wanted the love and support of my Mom and settled for whatever I could get. What child does not want to be loved and accepted even if it is dysfunctional? I did not know that I could charge Dad with abuse; I was unaware and blind to the fact. I was conditioned and taught, to believe that under no uncertain terms you respect your parents. I figured my Mom is the authority, she knows best, and she has my back. She wouldn't let any harm come to me - she is, after all, my Mother.

She wasn't there for me, didn't have Dad charged and arrested, and Dad came first. It was never talked about again and swept under the rug. It was the same for our relatives; they accepted what was and didn't question it. Only for the fact that Mom stayed with Dad, it led them to believe it wasn't as bad as they thought. Life went on; it was in the past and, even then, no one spoke to me to ask my side. Without any concern shown, they would shrug it off as if I didn't count. I thought I was never good enough, always tried to get Mom's approval, and was always trying to please. I've gone through my life having to prove myself time and time again. The stage set in motion, and from that moment on Dad's word prevailed over mine. If I didn't talk before, this further cemented my decision to stay quiet. Like the ancient ruins of Pompeii in Campania, Italy in 79 A.D., as Mt. Vesuvius erupted, I would seal up my past in a tomb of ash and pumice.

Tess and I split the rent; she bought her groceries, and I bought mine. I finally managed to buy a used car, and the TD Bank approved a loan since I was working at the Data Centre. Pretty good - I managed to do this at only 17! Strapped for money, and an easy fix, I survived on Campbell's chicken and rice soup. My supper every night was a bowl of soup and a piece of bread. My eating habits and nutrition were not priorities, and I didn't eat breakfast or lunch as I never got hungry. Besides, my tendency was not to cook since I didn't have the basic know-how or inclination to learn. My Mom didn't teach us or show us the basics of cooking. The only life skills I learned were by doing chores, cleaning the house, and ironing. I didn't have the money, know how to cook a proper meal, or, have the time. I would sometimes go to the convenience store located in the front of our apartment building and would treat myself to junk. That stopped when I found a chocolate bar crawling with worms one day. That was enough, and I thought, "Never again - I will not buy anything from this store again. This stuff is expired, and they sell it that way." Tess and I rarely saw each other. For the most part, she had her life, and I had mine, like two strangers passing in the night.

Tess became involved in a relationship, and not long after she would tell me, she was moving out. I didn't make enough money to pay the rent, not by myself, and ended up moving in with Norm and Janet, our old neighbors on Sprott Street. The arrangement was that I could rent a bedroom in their basement, and Janet would give me dinner. Even though Norm and Janet were very kind, my place was in the basement - nothing more.

Nine

The best thing to ever happen to me was the day I met Noah. At school, I had gone outside during recess for a smoke break, as I had done every day for the past two years. Noah, coming out one of the side doors, happened by chance to head my way. Locking eyes, in the spur of the moment, Noah started up a conversation. The attraction was instant, and Noah reminded me of a long-lost sailor, my soul mate from another time. Wearing white bell-bottom jeans, and a red militia shirt, a black bomber jacket filled out his skinny build. At 6'2" tall, he was clean cut with light brown hair, and his hazel brown eyes speckled with green. He offered me a cigarette and proceeded to pull his pack out from his pocket. We naturally started meeting at the same spot every day. He told me he was in the Reserves in the New Westminster Regiment and had started as a cadet. He would be shipped out to various Canadian Armed Forces bases across Canada and would take a leave from school for a couple of months for military training. I was living on Franklin Street as it turns out when Noah was at church every Sunday, just a block from where I lived. He would stop at the corner grocery convenience store located at the front of my apartment building almost every Sunday. All this time, our paths had crossed, and not once did we run into each other at the store.

Noah lived with his stepmother, Camille. He said, "My Dad

died in May 1979, of a heart attack, and he was only 54 years old." He was found slumped over the steering wheel, and the horn blaring caught the attention of passersby. Noah, stationed at a military base in Wainwright, Alberta, the Army called in the chaplain to tell Noah his Dad had died. He was then personally escorted to Edmonton and put on the first flight back to B.C. Delaying the plane; the passengers already boarded had to sit on the tarmac waiting for Noah's arrival. He was then driven home and given a military escort to his front door.

Noah went on to say, "My Mom lives in Victoria, but I don't talk to her." Proceeding to tell me of his bad childhood, he said, "Camille is more my mother, and she took me in at 15 years old when my parents divorced. My Dad married Camille soon after."

On our first date, Noah asked, "Do you want to see a movie?" and nodding, we took the bus to downtown Vancouver, to see National Lampoon's "Animal House." Arriving early, we stopped at McDonald's to grab a burger and fries. I have always been self-conscious, and had a complex about eating in front of people - so when Noah asked, "What do you want to eat?" I politely said, "Nothing, I'm not hungry."

Attending Burnaby North Secondary School, I was now in Grade 12 - 17 years old, and Noah was 18. We would hang out at my place after school until Janet confronted me. Belonging to the generation of being strict and old-fashioned, she said, "I will not condone your actions; it's not right or proper to allow your boyfriend into your room." What was I supposed to do? I was renting a room! I had no intention of following her "rules," and felt since I was paying rent, and on my own, had no right to tell me what to do! Still, having the utmost respect and gratitude for her, I said, "Thank you for letting me stay, but I'll be moving out." I rented a room at Julie Johnson's house, our friend from school. The same kind of situation, but her father didn't care who I brought home as long as I paid the rent.

A month or so into dating Noah, I was formally invited over to meet Camille. She was a minister, and the reverend of the Unity Church, a spiritualist church on Franklin Street. I was about to find out that she was a medium, originally from England. At first, all went quite well, and I told her I was in school, working, and living on my own.

At this juncture, I was becoming more attuned to my self-image, and not wanting rejection I improved my looks by changing my glasses to contact lenses and wearing makeup. As for eating, I could only say, "No thank you, I'm not hungry" so many times. Therefore, purging was my only answer; this would be my way of eating, being expected to eat, and not putting on the weight. I became quite adept at hiding it even from Noah. My insecurities became acute with the progression of our relationship. I was trying to get a sense of respect and self-worth and wanted only to be accepted. Purging boosted my confidence as I lost weight and became as skinny as a rail. It afforded me the luxury of wearing whatever I wanted to in any style of clothing. It wasn't that I was overweight but, I felt uneasy about myself and the way I looked; never thought I was good enough. For many years, I continued purging, and the only reason I stopped was when we started trying for a baby. Even then, it was not for my sake, but for the health of the baby.

For the most part, I was shy and had no self-confidence. A habit I picked up early on, was tucking my hands into my pockets everywhere I went; this was my security blanket that replaced sucking my thumb, which I didn't outgrow until I was a teen. When I was growing up, my Mom was not one to have the girl-to-girl talks, and there was no discussion about clothes, fashion or makeup. The norm was to make do or go without it. We didn't have the spare money to spend on extravagances. More often than not my Mom projected her insecurities on to us. Her complaints about her weight, her looks, her wrinkles, and her hair were commonplace. Then the "insults" came, critiquing my looks, and pointing out my imperfections. She, being so habituated to complaining gave no thought to how critical she had become. With no guidance, it was up to me to figure out what worked best for me.

One afternoon, Noah and I were sitting in Camille's living room when she said to both of us, "I don't know what your intentions are, but I expect Noah to finish Grade 12, and then he will go to trade school. Anything you have planned will have to wait." I was quite outspoken, and without hesitation, I blurted out, "why don't you ask Noah what he wants?" I didn't mean anything by it, and just figured Noah did have a say – besides, it was his life! In one quick motion, I was abruptly escorted to the door and told to leave. She didn't appreciate my "attitude," and even though Noah continued to see me, I wasn't welcome over anymore. One day, when I dropped Noah off at home, he was greeted at the front door by Camille, and she dropped a bombshell. She gave Noah an ultimatum, "You have a choice; you can stay and stop seeing her or, you will take your bags and leave." Noah's duffel bag already packed at the door. Noah, stumped by her sudden outburst, tried to size up her degree of seriousness. In a moment of decision, he grabbed his bag and moved in with me. I told Noah, "I can't support you; you'll have to get a job." With an ingenious, schooled attitude, Noah wore his military uniform to apply for a security guard position. The owner, a retired Army veteran, was quite impressed when Noah walked into the interview dressed in his military attire and promptly hired him on the spot.

Noah became disillusioned with school and thought it would be more advantageous to drop out. I stayed since I only had a month left before the end of Grade 12. School became mundane with Noah's absence, and I too dropped out. I still received my diploma though as I was only one credit short. A big milestone for me as I was the only one in my family to graduate. A couple of years later, Noah was successful in getting his diploma by correspondence. Through experience, he learned it wasn't too easy getting a job without it.

Our differences with Camille lasted for about a year and, because of it, Noah's family wasn't going to attend our wedding.

Earning minimum wage, we had very little money. Noah and his Dad both had the same name, so when a renewal for a Shell gas credit card came in the mail intended for Noah's Dad, Noah applied for it. It was approved, and we lived off of the Shell card for a few months. Always short of money, the Shell gas station was our one-stop shop for groceries and gas. We didn't ask our family for money or a hand-out. As time went by, we graduated to noodles and tomato sauce. Almost every night it would be our supper as it was the cheapest meal we could afford.

When Noah and I decided to get married, Noah had just turned nineteen. We picked my birthday, December 24th, for our wedding day as I thought with turning nineteen, I wouldn't need my parents' consent. We were wrong, and the priest informed us since the paperwork needed filing beforehand, I would still require my parents' consent.

We phoned around looking for a church that would marry us, but every priest refused and said, "Come back when you're older - you're too young." Finally, the priest at St. Michael's Church in Burnaby, agreed to meet with us. We arranged an appointment one evening to discuss our plans. It wasn't a good first impression when Noah and I went to the wrong church! Waiting for over an hour at the church two doors up, we ended up profusely apologizing, and explaining our mistake as to why we were so late. Thankfully, the priest was not upset and listened to our intentions to marry. The priest, a kindly, considerate, senior man, soon realized we were dead-set on getting married. Seeing how serious we both were, he agreed to perform the wedding. His one comment, "I suppose it's meant to be. It's not often I come across two people so young who are so determined." For the first time, I was in control of my life, and able to make my decisions. Finally, I had the upper hand, and my Dad was not going to walk me down the aisle! Noah and I exchanged our vows standing before the priest, and it was the happiest day of our lives. It felt so good to be in control.

During our reception, which we held in our apartment, Billy, my brother, decided it would be as good a time as any to confront Dad about the sexual abuse. Billy had already been drinking and, geared up with his sense of bravado, he was determined to show his brotherly ways. Locking himself and Dad in our bathroom, the confrontation halted our celebration as we all tried to get Billy to stop as it wasn't the time or place. Even though I didn't appreciate his timing, I felt honored that Billy was sticking up for me. Unfortunately, Dad was able to convince Billy that nothing happened, that it was all a lie, and Billy believed him. It was incredible! Not once did Billy ever approach me to get my side or even ask what had gone on. Once again, Dad's word prevailed over mine. Billy's actions pretty much put a wrench on our wedding day, and our sibling relationship strained from then on.

As a kid, I would go into Billy's bedroom when he wasn't home and poke through his stuff. My curiosity peaked, I only wanted some idea of who he was, his identity. Billy was hardly ever home and, when he was, it was only to tease or boss us around, especially while we were doing chores. With him being the only boy, he didn't have to do the household chores and it was left to the rest of us. Flipping through his record collection, I would select one, and listen to his type of music. I wasn't supposed to be in his room and, afraid of getting caught, I only stayed for a brief time. I looked up to Billy; after all, he was my older brother. We did not spend time together, and this was my way of getting to know him.

We spent our wedding night at a motel, and left in the morning for our honeymoon, driving to Reno, Nevada. We headed up the coast in the middle of winter and hit a snowstorm traveling through California. The radio issued a weather advisory to stay off the roads unless it was an emergency, but we were caught in the middle of nowhere in a blizzard and had no choice but to keep on going. Driving a couple of hours without seeing another car on the road was tense, but we thankfully made it without any mishaps.

Noah and I lived in the apartment across the hall from my Mom and Dad. It was the same apartment building my Mom and Dad were caretakers of in New Westminster, B.C., and Helen was still living at home. One particular night, Noah and I overheard shouting coming from their apartment. We stood in the hallway outside their door eavesdropping as we wanted to know what the commotion was all about. The shouting intensified and, still unsure, we quietly entered their apartment. Stunned, we stood silently trying to grasp the situation. Helen was pinned down, laid out on the floor, and Dad straddled over her slapping her across the face and upper torso. My Mom, standing on the sidelines, did nothing to interfere or stop the physical attack. I asked, "What's going on?" and my Mom shouted, "Stay out of it - she's got it coming to her." Helen was crying out and screaming for us to help.

Anger and disgust towards my Dad spewed forth, and I shouted, "That's enough!" My Dad, still in a frenzied state, and out of control, continued his onslaught. Tussling, we managed to break it up with some effort and got Helen to her feet. With a few more choice words exchanged, we took Helen with us and left the apartment. Glaring at my Mom and, still not brave enough to say it out loud, I thought with revulsion, "What's your excuse now!?"

From the first moment, I met Noah, he accepted me for who I was, as I did him in return. Together, we helped each other overcome our past, our childhood. I was not forthright in giving the facts of my abuse, and he only knew it happened. What was the point? - It happened, and I couldn't change the past. Not partial to seeking help, I kept it private and wanted above all to forget and look ahead instead. We never tried to control each other, and it would have been impossible to do so on both our sides.

Noah and I were two peas in a pod whereas I had my eating disorder and, Noah, had his self-destructive behavior. His coping mechanism for his insecurities was to obliterate his personal effects. One day, he took his watch and, placing it down on the cement, smashed it to smithereens with a rock. Quizzically I asked, "What are you doing?" and Noah replied, "I dunno, I just felt like doing it." Keeping up with my interrogation, I asked, "Why are you destroying your watch?" It was then he opened up, and matter-of-factly started telling me about his childhood. Three of his siblings were adopted out other than Cathy, the oldest, and Noah, the youngest. He would fall victim to his Mother's extreme physical and mental abuse. Cathy, being the favorite, didn't receive the same treatment Noah endured. Noah's Mother despised him and took out her hatred of him with acts of cruelty.

Noah would tell me different stories of the abuse his Mom inflicted on him. Once, when he was very young, it was during bath time, and his Mother without warning grabbed hold of him and forcefully held him under water. If it weren't for his Dad walking into the bathroom, Noah would have drowned. His punishment and torture included having his fingers slammed in the door for chewing gum, a knife jabbed into his stomach, and called "Dummy" while being hit with a hairbrush to the backside of his head. The abuse took place during the day while his Dad was at work. As well, his Mom would often pull him out of school to go and sell her homemade crafts door-to-door in downtown Vancouver. He would be absent from school a big portion of the year, leaving him to fall behind in his schoolwork.

It was only when Doris, Noah's Mom, had an extramarital affair with Lesley (Camille's husband at the time), Doris up and left with Lesley, and moved to Victoria, B.C. She disassociated herself from Noah but, one day right out of the blue phoned and asked him to come to Victoria for a visit. She said, "I'll pick you up at the ferry terminal." Noah's Dad dropped him off at the Horseshoe Bay Ferry Terminal, and Noah boarded the last ferry to Victoria. His Mom was not there to pick him up and, without knowing her phone number or address, Noah had to wait until morning to return to Vancouver. He spent the night sleeping on a bench outside the ferry terminal. At 14-years-old, Noah was just a pawn in her game of deception, and this would be the last time he heard from her until we were married. It wasn't until Noah went to stay with Camille at 15 years old, his life would turn around, and become stable. After the divorce, Doris married Lesley, and Noah's Dad married Camille.

Noah spent a lifetime trying to find the whereabouts of his other siblings - his two older brothers, and one older sister.

Hearing through the grapevine that Noah and I were married, Noah's Mom phoned to ask us to get together. Noah, susceptible to her scheming ways, fell into her trap. A cruel, malicious woman, I saw through her ploy, and her contrived sweetness and charm. After some discussion, and not trusting her intentions, Noah and I decided we were better off without her. I couldn't get over the fact that she had enough gall to think she could stroll right back into Noah's life after everything she put him through. She showed no remorse, gave no apology for her actions, and I wasn't about to let her hurt Noah again.

Back to the apartment in New Westminster. An episode that led to us evicted from our apartment was when we decided to bring home a puppy. The rules of the building were "No dogs allowed," and my Mom was adamant in saying, "You know the rules - get rid of the puppy or move!" Being stubborn, I said, "You have a dog; the owner won't find out, so why can't we have one? Besides, you let Tess stay in a vacant apartment for a couple of months without paying rent, and the owner didn't find out about that!" She would not budge, and within the week was showing our apartment to a listing agent without our consent. I arrived home from work and, as soon as I inserted the key in the door, my Mom greeted me. Belligerently, she said, "I showed your apartment today, and I've never been so humiliated in all my life!" Confused, I asked, "What are you talking about?" Ranting on, she stormed into our apartment, waving her arms in indignation. She said, "Look at this mess - how could you let it get so bad!?" Her final comment, "Clean this mess up. I want you out by the end of the month!" I couldn't understand why she was getting so upset. Yes, there was a mess - the puppy had got hold of the toilet paper, the newspaper we laid out, and a pillow. The chewed pieces are strewn about, but it wasn't that bad - at least, she hadn't dirtied. I resented her outburst and thought, "For crying out loud, puppies are going to make a mess. It's not like we live like this all the time!" The listing agent, appalled by the condition of the apartment, ridiculed my Mom, knowing full well I was her daughter. I got the brunt of my Mom's embarrassment, and she dished out her scorn. Hurt that my Mom couldn't stick up for me and tell the listing agent that she had the wrong idea - that it had just been an unfortunate accident. I had it cleaned up in five minutes, big deal right!? Besides, she had no right coming into our apartment without our consent. This confrontation resulted in us not talking for quite some time and moving out sooner than expected.

Noah and I didn't drink other than to have an occasional beer once in a while. I wouldn't entertain being around someone drunk, and it was a tendency I preferred to do without it. I had seen enough of alcoholism growing up, and would anxiously become nervous at the first sign of inebriation. It didn't help when we got invited to a party for Noah's 21st birthday. Spurred on to get drunk, he was handed one drink after another. Towards the end of the night, growing irritated by Noah's intoxication, I said, "Let's go - you've had enough!" Noah's first stop was to the bathroom upon arriving home where he vomited unceremoniously without cessation. Noah moaned he wasn't feeling good, and my only response was to say, "It serves you right - don't do it again!" I was still irate that he had chosen to drink so much.

Unfortunately, without mentioning any names, we were both introduced first to marijuana, and then to cocaine. It was at a time when Noah and I were trying to fit in, have a sense of belonging, and be a part of the flock. The marijuana I tried only once as I experienced hallucinations. The cocaine, on the other hand, opened me up. I was now able to talk without the usual shyness or inhibitions. The time came when both Noah and I decided to stop as the dependency was taking its toll. The effects of the drug resulted in us staying up all night and going to work the next morning with absolutely no sleep. Even though a weekend habit, we had become dependent, craved more, and it finally caught up. A very enjoyable, addictive drug, it was very hard to come away from but, after about a grueling month or so, we managed to ward off our addiction.

We turned to hiking instead, and it was our way of going in a more positive direction. Our first attempt, Dog Mountain in North Vancouver, was a strenuous workout! In a short time, we became quite the enthusiasts, traveling to Mount Baker in Washington on several excursions; Trophy Mountain in Clearwater; Golden Ears Provincial Park in Maple Ridge; Whistler, and North Vancouver. We had found a healthy way of releasing the daily pressures and stresses of our everyday life.

Now living on Adanac Street off Boundary Road in Burnaby, Noah had a strong desire to get a motorcycle. He went for his learner's, and our friend, Larry, helped coach Noah on how to ride. Our first argument arose when Noah persisted in wanting to purchase a brand-new Honda, Midnight Shadow, 750cc. My argument was we didn't have the money, so I said, "Make your choice; you can either buy a used car or buy the motorcycle. If you buy the motorcycle, it will be your only means of transportation - we can't afford both. You will have to drive it in the winter too or else take the bus." He purchased the bike and, true to his word, drove it in the winter months.

The exhilaration, the feel of the bike underneath me, and the rush were tantalizing. Now envious, my desire to own a motorcycle was motivation enough to get my learner's. Noah taught me with his bike, and I found I had a natural ability for riding a motorcycle. Even the immense size of Noah's bike wasn't enough to deter my determination. Picture this - a girl 5'5" tall, weighing about a 100 lbs., straddling a 750cc motorcycle. The sheer size of the bike alone was heavy enough that if I dropped it, I wouldn't have the muscles to pick it up! Borrowing Noah's motorcycle, I took my road test, and passed with flying colors on my first attempt without one mistake! At one point during the exam, doubt crept in, and I thought, "I can't do this." The instructor asked me to stabilize the motorcycle using the middle kickstand. Disheartened, I said, "I can't lift this motorcycle." He said, "I know - just show me the steps." I complied, and he nodded his approval. The instructor, going over the final checklist, commented, "You have a natural talent - you've done better than most of the men I've had in here. Here's your driver's license; you passed." I walked away beaming from head to toe. Not even Noah had passed on his first try, and I was in my glory!

Noah surprised me a week later by going out and buying me a used motorcycle. I was in awe and, best of all, the motorcycle was smaller, something I was more comfortable riding. It wasn't long before we had Helen and Tess, my sisters, addicted as well, and we would all take day trips cruising across the border.

One planned holiday, Noah and I decided to travel by motorcycle down the Oregon coast. Not the typical motorcycle enthusiasts outfitted in leather gear and accessories, we went as we were, and strapped on a backpack with a change of clothes. The first couple of days were wonderful, and we drove all day enjoying the freedom of being on a bike. The weather is cooperating, making it fun and pleasurable. Our luck was to change though as the clouds rolled in. At first, we thought, "It's okay; it's only a few sprinkles," but further down the highway, getting greeted with a downpour. Getting completely soaked, we stopped at a gas station to buy garbage bags, to wrap them around our feet and legs. Our idea didn't work, and we were completely drenched head to toe. It was a comical sight when at dusk, we pulled into the first motel we spotted along the way. Our clothes sopping wet, puddles of water collected beneath our feet, and the sounds of our water-logged runners sloshing with every step. Chilled to the bone, and shaking uncontrollably, we took turns in the tiny standup shower trying to warm up. Thank God for little miracles as we wrung out our clothes and shoes and strung them up to dry right beneath a ventilation fan blowing steady hot air. I have to say, after that day, we never took anything for granted, and we now know the meaning of the word comfort! It turned out to be one of the most memorable trips we had taken.

Spontaneity was our middle name, and we rented a car for a three-day long weekend excursion to San Francisco. The rental included unlimited mileage, so you can believe their shock when we returned the car on Monday, and they were astounded by the number of kilometers. Thinking they had made an error, they asked, "Where did you go? We can't figure out why the number of kilometers is so high."

We laugh now remembering our lack of judgment, preparedness, and our careless ways. Oh well, that's what we did; we took it as it came, and that's how we lived our lives.

We were eager to start our future and leave our past behind. We did not realize that we would have many more challenges ahead.

Noah

Walking through darkness, an empty shell
void of emotion I could not tell
that life would be heaven when you came to me
for you changed my life – always to be.
The moment we met, the image profound,
you reminded me of a sailor; I'd finally found.

You helped me along and cared for me,
you were my savior; no other could be.
Gently caressing like the ocean tide,
you carried away the pain inside.
Destiny foretold that you'd be mine;
soul mates from another time.
Your thoughtful ways, your special touch,
the way you know when life's too much.
Forever yours, from the day we met,
I love you, Noah, don't you forget.

Ten

Around ten years into our marriage, Noah and I bought our first house in Surrey, B.C. Scraping together a down payment of $2,500.00, we were enthralled by our accomplishment of owning a home and didn't care that it was a wartime bungalow. A 750- Sq. Ft. Two-Bedroom house, it was set up during the war to provide affordable temporary housing. The yard is what sold us on it, and the property had massive, giant evergreen trees sprawling the quarter acre lot. The first time my Mom and Victor (my second stepfather), dropped by to see the house right after we had moved in, she looked in horror, and her first comment was to say, "Oh my God, what have you done!?" She thought we had made the biggest mistake of our lives and wasn't at all impressed with the choice we made. Needless to say, five years later we sold, and more than doubled our initial investment.

One afternoon, I noticed a police car parked out front and, even though curious, I didn't speculate too much on it until there was a knock at our door. The policeman, introducing himself, handed me a subpoena. Shocked, I asked, "What's this for?" and he informed me that my stepfather, Boris Boiko, had charges laid, and I was being subpoenaed to testify. My mouth dropped open, and I shrieked, "Do I have a choice - what happens if I don't testify?" He said, "You will be getting arrested. I need to come in and get your statement." I wasn't prepared to have this thrown into my lap without any warning. I thought, "I don't want any part of this - I want to forget my past; this is private, and the last thing I want to do is talk about it!" The policeman said, "Take a few moments to collect your thoughts, but I will need to come in and take your statement." With no choice, I sat down and gave my detailed statement. Moved by my answers, the policeman tried to keep his composure, and in the end politely said, "Thank you for your time, I'm sorry."

I went to the Courthouse and only showed up right at the appointed time to give my testimony. An open courthouse trial allowed the public access to walk in and watch the proceedings. Upset by this, I thought, "This is ludicrous - do I not get any rights whatsoever!?" I approached one of the lawyers and said, "Can I close the doors? I don't want everybody in here when I testify." He replied, "No, you're not allowed to close the doors; they have to stay open." Indignant, I thought, "No way - I am not doing this, not in front of everyone." I motioned family members aside and said, "If you want me to testify, you had better close the doors, stand outside, and block anyone from coming in. That's the only way I'm doing this." They did.

During my testimony, the court broke for lunch, and I had to wait for the court proceedings to resume before finishing my testimony. Tess and Helen, along with her friends (there for emotional support), decided to go and grab lunch, and Tess asked if I wanted to go. I said, "No," and proceeded to walk over to the seating area. My Mom, reluctant on leaving me alone, stood hesitantly debating her next move. Containing my vehemence, I said, "Go with them - I want to be alone." Sensing my emotional distress, she thought it wise to stay with me. We sat silently and didn't exchange any words. I was in no shape for chitchat as wave after wave of emotions coursed through me. I thought, "I have to be strong" and, with all my will, I fought to keep control. There was absolutely no way I was going to show my emotions -not in front of Mom. I thought, "You weren't there for me before, so don't pretend to be here for me now." I finished my testimony once again without the "onlookers," and walked out. I didn't stick around to await the outcome. I would later learn that my Dad was found guilty and sentenced.

By this point in time, my Mom and Dad divorced. He was

having an extramarital affair with Ellen from work, and my Mom found out. The marriage was over and, shortly after, my Mom met Victor, Ellen's husband. My Dad ended up marrying Ellen, and my Mom married Victor. There again, the switching of the spouses!

I never thought I should have to defend myself, explain myself - never did and never will. I knew I was telling the truth. The problem with that was, no one else knew. It would always be my Dad's word against mine. I thought, "At the very least, I don't have to put up with Dad anymore." Victor was an alcoholic too but, if you must compare, he at least was a better father figure than the other two had been.

Always in the back of my mind, I wondered about my biological father, Peter. The five "W's" - Who, what, when, where, and why constituted my basic need to find out the complete story. I wanted to know if he had any regrets, had ever looked for us or even wanted to. In some respects, my feelings of abandonment, separation, acceptance, and belonging were similar to those felt by adoptees. Never pursuing it further, I found out a few years later that he was a long-time resident of Rossland, B.C. It turns out; he hadn't changed his ways; he was still an abusive alcoholic and lived alone. He hadn't amounted to much over the years and didn't remarry or have any more children. It wasn't the good ending I was hoping for, but it put to rest any notions of getting in contact with him. It would have been nice though to go to Rossland under a cloak of secrecy and observe this man who was my father.

Whenever my Mom thought Dad was having an affair, she would confront him with her suspicions. One particular day, she snapped and lost control. Her mental state was one of desperation and despair, pushing her to her limits, and she stormed out of the house. Frantic to get away, to escape, she grabbed the keys to the Cadillac to leave. With all of us chasing behind, we tried to block her leaving, and screamed for her to stop. Exasperated, she yelled, "Get out of the way!" and screeched out of the driveway. Worried about her frame of mind, I raced to my car and, with Tess coming with me, we followed in hot pursuit. At breakneck speeds, she drove like a madman playing a reckless game of cat and mouse. At one point, becoming concerned with our safety as well as others', I slowed down. We lost sight of her and trailed further behind.

At other times, she would ask me to follow Dad, to see if I could find out if he were meeting someone and fooling around. I would get in my car, park up the street out of sight, and wait for Dad to leave home. After a couple of unsuccessful attempts, I gave up. I could never catch him. Obviously, he took a different route or had caught onto our guise of deception.

There would be another suicide attempt, with my Mom taking a large dosage of pills, Anacin to be exact; this derived from the fact that she was certain Dad was having another affair. I drove her to Royal Columbian Hospital, but she refused to go in. We walked up and down alongside the hospital grounds, and I was diligent in observing her condition for any worsening signs of decline. Complaining she wasn't feeling good, I told her to vomit to bring up the pills. I waited and watched knowing if her condition worsened, we were right outside the hospital.

We didn't have the typical Mother and Daughter relationship. Subconsciously, after Melanie died, I lived with the fear. Afraid, I was vigilant in making sure no one else would die by suicide. That is why I continued and didn't just walk away - she needed someone to look after her.

I have never been one for bragging about myself and was never interested in being in the limelight or getting recognition. I swayed away from it and wasn't comfortable with the idea of being the center of attention. I have never made a good first impression, but one value I did possess was honesty. In the hopes of finding a job after I was laid-off, I obtained the services of a Personnel Agency. The economy had taken a downturn, and jobs were hard to obtain. After the usual questions in the interview, she then asked, "What experience do you have?" I replied, "Accounting," and she countered, "Where did you go to school to get your degree?" I remarked, "I didn't go to school; I taught myself." Well, the interview was over as she abruptly brushed me off, and it was apparent she did not want to waste any more of her time. Standing up to dismiss me, she stated, "You need to undergo a screening test to evaluate your skills," and I responded boldly with, "Okay, I'll take the test right now." After completing the test, I was getting called back in. A different approach now, as she commented, "You have a remarkable test result - your scores are one of the highest I have ever seen." She was now quite interested in placing me with a firm.

The one question remains, "How did I get through it?" Simply put, "I never gave up." Point-blank, I looked at the good, not the bad - the bad I tucked away. I would never have made a good lawyer; my tendency is to see all sides. As the saying goes, "Don't judge someone until you've walked a mile in their shoes." Growing up, I chose to see the good - not concentrate on the bad and kept hoping circumstances would change and get better over time.

After the court case, my Mom told me of the time when she first became involved with Dad. She said, "Dad's ex-wife phoned, and warned me, 'If you have daughters, I suggest you be careful. Previously Boris has been charged with indecent exposure, and I think you need to be concerned'". My Mom said, "I thought she was just spiteful, and seeking revenge. I guess I should have listened."

Eleven

Flying over the rooftops, the stork carries the newborn in a cloth bundle, then lands at the doorstep of the waiting happy couple. Oh my, if only making babies was as simple as the popular fable of the stork delivering babies to waiting parents!

At first, Noah and I were not ready to have children and, at that point in our lives, motherhood was not a priority. I was on birth control pills, and we had enough gumption to think we took all the necessary steps to prevent an unwanted pregnancy. It worked, and I did not become pregnant.

We started thinking about having a baby when I was around 23 years old. We tried to conceive, but after a few months, we were unsuccessful. Frustrated and disappointed, I made an appointment with a gynecologist, Dr. Pano. While performing a laparoscopy, the doctor found a blockage in both my tubes and some scar tissue. Not overly concerned, she said, "Keep trying and start a schedule. Take your temperature, keep a record and, within the two days of ovulation every month, make a point of having intercourse. Try this for a few months and see if it works." After more failed attempts, she referred us to Dr. Deere, a fertility specialist in Vancouver. At a loss, she said, "Maybe Noah has a problem." Again, after a series of tests, it was then detected that Noah had a varicocele condition that causes low sperm count, and he would require surgery. Initially, Dr. Deere was quite hopeful that our infertility problems were solved and recommended fertility treatment by artificial insemination. Unfortunately, after many treatment cycles using Noah's sperm, I still could not conceive. Desperate, we even tried donor insemination as an alternative thinking that might work.

In April of 1993, Noah entered a contest through work to win a free, all-inclusive trip for two to anywhere in the world that Air Canada flew. Noah won the tickets and, after some conflict with work as to whether he was entitled to have entered the contest, we were on our way to Rome, Italy. We traveled to Italy, then on to France and, lastly, to Switzerland. Arriving in Rome, we stayed in a quaint motel room that gave a bird's eye view of the rustic day-to-day lives of the people behind the scenes - it was so picturesque. We ventured by train to the medieval town of Lucca. The entire town surrounded by a stone wall built in the 1500s. Arriving quite late at night, we found the streets quiet and deserted. Wandering up and down the cobblestone streets, looking for a place to eat, only succeeded in getting us lost completely. Finally, after an hour or so of searching, we stumbled upon a hotel, checked in, and by this point were too exhausted to eat. Noah's customary habit was to inspect the room. The spacious suite adorned with classy, elegant decor of the highest quality, and the elaborate bathroom was laid out in marble-tiled floors and walls. Noah, noticing a gold, tasseled rope hanging from the tiled wall beside the claw-foot bathtub, started tugging on it to figure out why it was there. The front desk, a moment later phoned and asked, "Is everything okay?" and Noah replied, "Yes." The front desk repeated, "Are you sure you don't need help?" and puzzled, Noah, asked unequivocally, "No, why do you ask?" The front desk replied, "You are ringing for help." Stumped and mystified, Noah couldn't understand what he was saying. Finally, the front desk stated, "The tasseled rope in the bathroom is for emergencies only, and you only pull it if you require help." Noah and I broke into hysterical laughter after hanging up the phone. Noah had thought the tasseled rope was to help old people up who had difficulty getting out of the tub. He kept pulling and pulling on it and had become quite methodical in his efforts to figure out how it worked. Imagine the surprise of the front desk when the alarm kept sounding off, and they really must have thought someone was in dire need.

Easter Sunday, we went to the Vatican to attend Easter Mass, and to watch Pope John Paul II give Easter service. Noah videotaped the procession of the Pope entering into the Vatican until a couple of nuns came rushing over. Waving their arms in protest, they said in a hushed, urgent Broken English whisper, "Turn off your camcorder; it is not allowed."

From Italy, we crossed over to France, whereby the train was stopped at the border crossing to inspect for illegal drug trafficking and smuggling. The Italian border patrol boarded the train armed with machine guns and escorted by trained German Shepherd dogs. Their demeanor was stern and businesslike as they were searching everyone's passport. Not speaking or understanding Italian were not in your favor. It was quite a culture shock and, even in Rome, the militia stood guard at almost every corner. The same level of security when you entered the bank. You couldn't just walk through the second door entrance; you needed to be buzzed in to gain entry into the bank. If you carried a backpack, you were refused entry, which was our case. Noah denied entry whereby the staff ignored him and refused to buzz him through. Noah threw up his hands in frustration and, ultimately, a customer noticing his predicament, pointed to his backpack and said, "You must leave it outside; that is why they won't let you in." A trip well worth taking, and a once in a lifetime chance as we would never have been able to afford this on our accord.

Resuming fertility treatment when we returned home, I became pregnant at 35 years old. Our ordeal lasted a long ten years. Our good fortune did not last though, and at 12-weeks' gestation, I started bleeding. Dr. Pano performed an emergency ultrasound and, not hearing a heartbeat, she said, "I'm sorry, you've lost the baby, and you have miscarried." Confused and reluctant to accept her devastating news, I asked, "What do you mean, how?" She said, "You've had a spontaneous abortion - I don't know why. I will schedule a D&C for you today, and you will need to go to the hospital. It needs to be done right away as I'm concerned about your health." Too distraught, I replied, "No, I won't, not today." In complete denial, I laid awake that night sobbing and crying, inconsolable, unwilling, and unable to accept the fact that I had lost our "little one" inside. I was devastated and felt I had failed. It wasn't until the next morning Noah came to me and, in his gentle way, said, "We have to go to the hospital - you have no choice. We must go; you need the D&C."

It had already been over ten years of trying to have a baby, and we had pursued every option available to us. We even went to a fertility clinic in Seattle, Washington, for a second opinion. We were getting told in our case that our chances were slim, and it would probably be a waste of time and money to continue. After several more unsuccessful attempts, Dr. Deere suggested we try a new fertility clinic that just opened up in Vancouver, called Future Fertility Centre. One more time, we had hope. At this point, we were growing despondent, and our family suggested we give up. Noah and I weren't about to do that, and thought, "We are going for it, even if the chances are slim."

Future Fertility Centre opened in 1996 and provided the latest assisted reproductive technology of In-Vitro Fertilization in the Lower Mainland. Our initial consultation with Dr. Al Knowne, began January 12, 1997, and after a complete diagnosis, told that both of us had fertility problems. Noah's consisted of poor motility and low sperm count, and I was not producing enough mature eggs. Dr. Knowne informed us our rate of success in conceiving was minimal, but even still to give it a try.

He suggested we start with the less expensive alternative of Intrauterine Insemination (IUI), a procedure whereby your partner's sperm will be washed and prepared, and then inserted into the cervix near the top of the uterus – thus, giving it the best chance of fertilizing an egg. All our efforts were ineffective, and I could not become pregnant. Getting very frustrated, we consulted with Dr. Knowne in May 1998, for more advice. Our next step would be to try Intracytoplasmic Sperm Injection (ICSI). A specialized form of In-Vitro Fertilization, this procedure would cost approximately $6,000.00, plus the drug expense. We emptied our RRSP accounts and savings to pay for it as we were not ready to throw in the towel.

At this time, Noah and I were living in Mackenzie, B.C. Noah's work transferred him in April 1997, and we were commuting to Vancouver for treatment. I ended up staying with Camille, my mother-in-law, in Ladner for the duration of the new treatment, and Noah stayed in Mackenzie, commuting when needed. A more complicated procedure as many more steps were involved.

The first step on my part was to start daily injections of fertility drugs to stimulate my ovaries into producing mature eggs. I did this at home for about 8 to 10 days, then went for blood work and ultrasounds to monitor if I had any eggs. If so, to find how many eggs, and if they were suitable for retrieval. Noah's sperm was then taken to the lab to isolate as much healthy moving sperms as possible, then washed and prepared for fertilization. The embryologist then carefully injects each selected egg with a single sperm. The injected egg is then put into an incubator and checked the next day for signs of fertilization. On May 31, 1998, I had three embryos transferred inside of me, and it was quite an accomplishment since I only had five eggs in total.

At 36-years-old, Noah and I received the news treatment had worked - it was a success, and I was pregnant! The estimated due date was March 6, 1999, and we were elated.

After receiving an ultrasound in the weeks to come, we learned we were expecting twin boys. A miracle - not only was I pregnant, but we were having twins! I went back to Mackenzie, and Dr. Lindsay, an Obstetrician, monitored my pregnancy.

At 22 3/7 weeks' gestation, I ran into complications and started bleeding. Admitted to Mackenzie Hospital on November 6, 1998, I was having some contractions and was in premature labor. A cervical cerclage surgery was going to be performed on November 7, 1998, as my cervix had opened up, and was already 2 cm dilated. A cerclage is a stitch to hold the cervix closed. Unfortunately, soon after, I developed a urinary tract infection caused by the surgery, and my cervix had opened up. Mackenzie Hospital did not have the specialized intensive care required to handle my pregnancy at such an early stage and told that if I could make it to 23 5/7 weeks' gestation, I would receive approval for transfer by B.C. Women's Hospital in Vancouver. I would not be accepted before that as the chances of survival were slim to none. To try and stop the contractions, I was given magnesium sulfate intravenously. Before long, I was having difficulty breathing and, with the symptoms worsening, I buzzed for the on-duty nurse. Thinking I was hyperventilating, and having a panic attack, she said, "Just calm down and breathe" while handing me a paper bag, and then she left. One more time, I called for the nurse and, this time was more insistent by saying, "I don't have panic attacks - I just can't breathe." Condescendingly, she conceded and called in the doctor on duty. A few minutes later, the doctor, after checking my breathing, put me instantly on oxygen. I was in pulmonary edema and was taken off the medication immediately. He informed me, "You are one of very few that has this reaction to this drug." Shamefaced and noncommittal, the nurse returned to her duties. Under complete bed rest, I was instructed not to push under any circumstances as my cervix had once more opened up. The night before I was getting transferred to B.C. Women's Hospital, the contractions and back pain intensified, and I could do nothing but writhe in agony. I have always been one to handle pain, but now I was at my limit. The pain was so excruciating; I had no choice but to tell Noah to go home when he showed up after work. I can't take much more; I need to concentrate, and try to zone out if I can." Zoning out is a technique I use to fight through the pain. I focus all my thoughts and energy on floating away - almost like an out-of-body experience. Through this, I can project myself into a state of unconsciousness. Throughout the night, I did my best to block out the pain mentally and, by morning, it had subsided somewhat.

I was relieved on November 17, 1998, the next day, to find out the approval for transfer had come, and I was to be flown by Air Ambulance later in the afternoon. Noah couldn't come with me as there wasn't enough room on the plane. Landing at Vancouver International Airport, I was taken by ambulance the rest of the way. On a stretcher in the ambulance, I was bursting to go to the bathroom. The ambulance attendant told me my only option was to use a bedpan. I said, "I'm not using a bedpan when everyone can see me through the back window." Smiling, he said, "It's a one-way window; no one can see in." I thought, "Nope, can't do it; it's too unnerving." With a stubborn reserve, I said, "I'll wait," I was admitted straight away by Janice, the attending nurse at B.C. Women's Hospital. Laid out on the stretcher, I arduously told her, "I have to go the bathroom!" and she replied, "Yes, of course, but first let's examine you." With one look, she exclaimed, "You are about to deliver - the baby is already coming out!" She quickly handed me the bedpan and said, "You have to go in here; you can't go to the bathroom - the baby may fall out." Looking back, I guess it was a good thing I didn't go to the bathroom in the ambulance. They would not have been equipped to deal with my premature delivery.

Calling the doctor over, they rushed me to the delivery room. Dr. Williamson, the attending doctor, briefly introduced himself, and said, "I'm sorry, we have no time to waste - we have to do this now!" I had a vaginal birth, and he said, "When I tell you to push, you push, and keep pushing until I tell you to stop." Our first baby, Lucas, was delivered at 7:20 p.m. A glimmer of hope as he tried to take his first breath, but he wasn't able. Janice carried him quickly to an adjoining room, and I could see she was using a straw to try and help him breathe. She was unable to resuscitate him, and Lucas, our first-born son, was pronounced dead at 7:30 p.m. He weighed only 590 grams. Our second son, Matt, was delivered at 7:27 p.m. He weighed only 495 grams, but at least he was breathing. I got to hold both our babies only for an instant as Matt need to be rushed to the Neonatal Intensive Care Unit and placed in an incubator. We would now be transferred over to Children's Hospital. I was in anguish, and alone. Everything happened so quickly, and, in shock, I had no time to react or comprehend. Distraught, I only wanted Noah to be there, but I was on my own. Right away, I knew I had to phone Noah and let him know. I tried to get hold of him at home, but I suddenly realized this was the evening he was taking a night course. Again, nothing was going right, and I had no choice but to phone my Mom and get her to contact Larry, Noah's boss.

He would have to go down to the school and pull Noah from class. For over an hour, I waited for Noah to call and, filled with dread, I relayed the terrible news. Noah took the first flight out from Mackenzie and arrived the next morning. That night, I numbly went through the motions as the shock had not subsided. More than anything, I wanted Noah here - but that was out and, whether I liked it or not, I had to wait till morning. My Mom arrived, and, with impatience, I told her to leave. I was not in the mood for company and did not have the strength to put on pretenses. She commented, "I don't know if I should stay. Victor has to go to work in the morning," That was enough to put me on edge. Then Tess showed up, followed by Cindy, my sister-in-law.

"Tell them to get out - I don't want to see them right now," I told my mom. It didn't go over too well. Then I thought, *give me a break - I have just flown in to Vancouver, found out I was in labor, lost our baby, our other son is in ICU, and Noah's not here!* I wasn't concerned about hurting their feelings, and I just needed some time alone - at the very least, enough to absorb and process the whirlwind of events.

I was in a state of self-preservation, and their timing couldn't have been more inappropriate. I visited Matt in ICU several times that night until visiting hours were over and then laid awake the entire night.

I was unaware that the nursing staff had placed a placard outside my door to identify the loss of our baby, and to show discretion. Given a private room, all I could hear were the joyous celebrations of other parents and family members as they welcomed their new addition. Feeling very isolated, it took all my willpower to walk down the corridors and pretend all was well. Feeling self-conscious, I did not want to stick out like a sore thumb, have them point and, in a hushed gossip, say, "Oh, that's the one that lost her baby - poor thing, she had twins."

With the utmost respect and consideration, Sarah, the nurse on duty, brought Lucas, our son, to my room. Wrapped in a blanket, as if he was still alive, she placed him in Noah's arms. With an overwhelming sense of loss and sadness, we cried. After a time of consoling each other, I took Noah to ICU to see Matt. Still, in serious condition, all Noah could do was place his hand inside the incubator to touch Matt gently, and only for a few minutes.

The only consolation was whenever we asked to see Lucas, our first baby, Sarah would oblige and bring him into our room. With the utmost compassion, she would feign affection, and give the pretense that all was well. She gave us our respect, honored our grieving process and, with it, a comfort I will not forget. I have nothing but admiration for her as it takes a special person to partake in such a difficult task, to carry a deceased baby and show no signs of revulsion. Even up to our last request to see Lucas, Sarah came back to my room, and with empathy said, "I'm sorry; I don't suggest you see your baby anymore." We

questioned her further, not understanding until she replied, "It wouldn't be wise; I'm sorry, but decomposition is starting to set in."

We continued our vigilance with Matt, and every moment filled with apprehension and hope. The doctors were doing all they could but, on the morning of November 19, 1998, two doctors knocked at my door. The one doctor said, "Matt is hemorrhaging; it's in his brain. We're sorry, he isn't going to make it, and there is nothing more we can do. We need you to come to ICU, and you will have to make the decision to take him off life support. Right now, we have him on morphine to help ease the pain, but he's suffering. The sooner you can come, the better." The heartbreak, so immediate, it felt as if my heart was being ripped out and pulled apart.

The nurse escorted us to a private Grieving Room, where both Lucas and Matt were then quietly carried into us. The nurse said, "I'll leave you alone; take all the time you need and, when you are ready, come and get me." Noah and I took this time, this private time, to cradle our babies, and immerse ourselves within the limited amount of time left. Trying to fit a lifetime of love, happiness, and nurturing into this small, precious window of time - the mental image ingrained for what should have been the happiest time of our lives but, instead, having to say goodbye to both our beautiful baby boys.

Upon returning, the nurse, with heartfelt compassion, said, "If you are unable to go through with this, I fully understand, and I will carry it out for you if you wish." I replied, "No, I will do this; it's up to me, and I need to be the one." Holding both our babies in my arms, the nurse unplugged the life support, and quietly left the room. With Noah by my side, I held Lucas and Matt until Matt died. All within a mere few minutes and, as he clutched hold of my finger in his tiny hand, he took his last and final breath. November 19, 1998, at 12:36 p.m. is when Matt died - the burden and pain so intense, we couldn't bear it. One more time, Noah and I endured the heartache of now losing our second son. We stayed in the confines of the private room and held our babies as the unrelenting wave of loss and emptiness consumed us. I never in my life thought it would come to this.

I was still a patient and was expected to stay for a couple more days before getting released. Sarah dropped by my room to check on me, and the moment she asked, "How are you doing?" a flood of emotion overtook me. Gripped in a vortex of release so absolute, and without any words exchanged it was like every ounce of my bottled-up emotions were exploding and bursting. I couldn't stop the outpour and, with it, the uncontrollable crying. Without a doubt I knew, Sarah was sent to comfort me. I had always kept my emotions in check, but Sarah was the only one with whom it seemed I couldn't control the tidal wave. A very spiritual release and I could see in her eyes the deep, meaningful connection - the compassion and understanding so absolute, it was like an angel had been sent to help me.

Noah arranged the funeral, and we had the service at Forest Grove Cemetery; Melanie buried at the same cemetery. We cremated Lucas and Matt, placing them together, and placed my crucifix atop their ashes. After the service, Noah and I stood alone at the gravesite, torn, not wanting to leave our babies behind. We stood deep in timeless thought reliving our loss and, when we turned to leave, a brilliant double rainbow appeared overhead. It was as if it was meant for us, a sign that filled us both with a sense of peace.

I learned from Dr. Williamson a cerclage should have been performed as soon as possible, especially since I was pregnant with twins. He said, "It may have helped in preventing your loss. Next time make sure it gets done." He added, "You are at high risk and, if you get pregnant again, you should stay in Vancouver." Having only the highest regard and gratitude for Dr. Williamson, I asked him if he would be my doctor if we decided to try again; I respected and valued his opinion.

Noah and I flew back to Mackenzie within the week and grieved alone. The coming year was the most difficult time, as grief, hopelessness, and despair filled us; after everything we had been through, how could this happen to us, we were so confused; are we not meant to have children?

All hope is slipping away, and I contemplated suicide. I wanted nothing more than to be with Lucas and Matt. I came to the decision that I would take an overdose of pills while Noah was at work.

The next day, I sat cross-legged on the floor and emptied out all the medications given to me by the hospital. Despondent, I sat in a trance staring at the pills I held cupped in my hand. I even went as far as to pop them into my mouth, and waning, I spat them back out. *No, I can't. No matter how much I want to be with Lucas and Matt, I can't leave Noah; he needs someone too,* I thought. It was enough for me to pull myself together and gather up my strength not to give up.

It was almost a year before we contemplated trying again. One more time; if it doesn't work this time, that will be it. No more - we can't take any more. We agreed. After 13 years, we were giving up hope of ever having children. We had considered adoption, even went as far as inquiring, but were told we would have difficulty as the waiting list was long and we were too old.

Our Little Babies

Even though they were sick, I didn't see,
for only their beauty shone through to me

Lucas, our first, tried to hold on, so true,
he stayed blocking the womb,
so, he wouldn't fall through.

Taking only one breath when he was born,
 he tried again for some.
The second wouldn't come.

I held Lucas only after he died,
and for a moment ... he looked at peace,
to be alive, then it ceased.

Matt, our second, stayed for two days,
clenching my finger in his little hand so
he never let it go.

He tried to open his eyes,
to see,
but he was just too young, for it to be.

Not alone,
I held Matt until he died,
in my arms – Noah by my side.

Both were fighters,
 too much to bear,
struggled to hold on, life isn't fair.

Our two little babies, the brief time we had
The joy of being a Mother, I felt so much,
love so strong with just your touch.

Heaven sent for only six months,
too soon, I cry,
"Our babies we love, oh why?"

Twelve

On March 21, 1999, at 37 years old, we went for our second cycle of treatment at Future. Once more, I had five eggs, and three embryos transferred. We kept our fingers crossed. We were thrilled when we found out that I was pregnant again with twin boys! Because I was high risk, I had no option but to go to Vancouver and stay there for the duration of my pregnancy. Not to repeat myself again, but I was once more under the care of Dr. Williamson at B.C. Women's Hospital. The first thing he did was to put a stitch in my cervix. My estimated due date was December 24, 1999, the same day as my birthday and, as it turned out, Dr. Williamson's birthday too! Noah stayed in Mackenzie as he had to work, and every so often he made the trip to Vancouver to visit me.

Unfortunately, Dr. Williamson ended up taking a leave of absence halfway through my pregnancy, and I would get transferred to Dr. Justice as a patient. I had such bad morning sickness and was having a difficult time carrying the weight. Not only did I have back pain, but my legs and feet were swelling up as well. Dr. Justice said, "You need to slow down and, if you can, stop working and get some rest. I'll send you to a Nutritionist; she may have some ideas of what can help nausea." In meeting with the Nutritionist, she questioned my eating habits. After giving her a list of my daily intake, she said, "You're eating right, but it's not enough." I replied, "I don't get hungry," and she answered, "You must be one of those people who doesn't require a lot of calories." She suggested, "Eat more protein, buy cheese, and crackers will help with the morning sickness. Break it up, eat more often, and eat smaller portions throughout the day. That will help a lot with the morning sickness.

Otherwise, you're doing fine."

I took their advice, stopped working, and became a "couch potato." I had to be careful, not overdo it, and get some rest. Still quite apprehensive and afraid, I held my breath praying nothing was going to go wrong this time.

At close to 30 weeks' gestation, I ran into complications. Speaking with Dr. Justice, she said, "There is a problem; your ultrasound is showing that one of your twins is not growing as he should. The increase in his growth rate now is only half what it should be. It doesn't make any sense. Going by the previous ultrasounds, they were both progressing, and their weight and growth were fine. For some inexplicable reason, the placenta is not providing the same food and oxygen that it did before. The one twin is fine, but it's the health of the other twin, I'm concerned. We could leave it, and just continue to monitor the situation or, we can proceed with an emergency caesarean. Either way, there will be risks. I think it's necessary to admit you now as you need to be on complete bed rest." Without warning I was getting admitted to the hospital. Dr. Justice continued by saying, "Let's monitor you for the time being; it will give me time to start steroid injections to improve the babies' lungs. Right now, they are too immature."

With steady monitoring, it became apparent that to avoid any more distress or complications, Dr. Justice had to decide whether or not to proceed with an emergency caesarean. First, though, she needed to get my stitches out. Taking me to a clinic room, she tried to cut out the sutures and, with each attempt, it started bleeding out. Growing impatient, she said, "If you bleed out anymore I'll have to take you to surgery," and a few seconds later, asked, "What was Dr. Williamson thinking? He sure put them in tightly; I can't believe I'm having such a difficult time getting them out." Smiling, I replied, "At least, they stayed in - that's all I care about." Finally managing to cut the remaining stitches out, at 34 weeks, I was headed for the operating room at six weeks premature. A spinal tap (a medical procedure in which a needle gets inserted into the spine), needed to be done for anesthesia. I was placed in a sitting position and told to bend my head and shoulders forward. The nurse asked Noah to help by holding my shoulders and making sure I stayed still and didn't move. Starting the procedure, the nurse ran into difficulty inserting the needle. She kept saying to Noah, "You need to hold her still." Glancing at Noah, she asked, "Are you okay? You look like you're going to pass out." Sure enough, the sight of blood, my blood, made Noah turn a pale, ghostly white, and he was ready to faint. It struck me funny as Noah, having been a First Aid Responder and a Volunteer Fireman, dealt with medical emergencies all the time, but I guess this was too close to home. Another nurse took over, and the spinal tap went without a hitch. The nurse even remarked, "You sure can take a lot of pain; I didn't even need to hold you - you're doing fine."

Getting prepped for surgery, a nurse entered the room and, brimming with uncontained excitement, asked, "Remember me?" Puzzled, I could only look at her as she continued, "I was the nurse on duty a year ago when you came in. I was the one holding your hand." Instant recollection as I said, "Yes, I remember you, but you look different." She replied, "You're right" and, showing me her I.D. badge; she had indeed changed her hairstyle. Janice went on to ask, "Do you know where you are?" and, again, I just looked at her. She responded, "You're in the same room as you were before!" I couldn't believe the coincidences. What were the odds of the same events happening the second time around?

This time though, Noah was with me in the operating room. Colin was born at 6:16 a.m., weighing 2,485 grams and, two minutes later at 6:18 a.m., weighing 1,545 grams, came Logan. It was three days before Lucas and Matt were born a year ago, November 14, 1999. Colin and Logan are fraternal twins, meaning not identical, just like Lucas and Matt.

Noah, eager to record the birth of Colin and Logan, took his camera out but, when he started snapping pictures, the camera wouldn't work. Baffled, he said, "I don't know what's going on; I had checked the camera before I came, and it was working fine." Even the nurse gave it a try but couldn't find the problem. She said, "I'm sorry, I don't even have the spare camera; for some reason, it's not here in the drawer where it's supposed to be." The odd thing was when we got home and checked the camera, there was no malfunction, and it was working fine.

I was conscious throughout the surgery; my view obstructed by a drape. Towards the end of surgery, I unintentionally saw the aftermath of what a caesarean involved. It was now my turn to almost faint! The incision, still wide open, gave me a front row seat to the blood-soaked dressings, the excess blood spilling out and onto the floor - and my organs were visible. The used dressings were piled haphazardly in buckets beside the operating table. It wasn't a pleasant sight, and I turned my attention elsewhere.

Colin and Logan were immediately taken to Intensive Care and placed into incubators. Painstakingly, we waited, hoping the outcome would be favorable as Colin and Logan were six weeks premature. Our ordeal was far from over, and there were many more obstacles to overcome. Colin's assessment included respiratory problems, and Logan suffered an intraventricular hemorrhage a week after birth, bleeding in the brain - both systematic due to prematurity. The synchronicities between Lucas and Matt, and Colin and Logan were striking. Colin had respiratory problems and, Lucas, also our first born, was not breathing. Logan had an intraventricular hemorrhage a week after being born, and Matt also had a brain hemorrhage soon after being born. It was unmistakable how uncanny these two parallels were.

With further testing, the diagnosis was that Logan had cerebral palsy. During the consultation with a Neurologist, her predictions were favorable, and the only disappointment was he would more than likely have a difficult time in sports. We didn't care and were only grateful that Logan was alive. We could deal with anything else and felt so blessed to have two beautiful little boys.

Another chance meeting would occur while walking down the hospital corridor. We passed Sarah in the hall, the same nurse we had a year ago when we lost Lucas and Matt. In the very same instant, we both noticed each other and turned around. It was such a comfort to see her again and bring her up-to-date on what had transpired.

For some reason, when I started breastfeeding I was unable to produce milk. With the help of a lactation specialist, I tried a new trial drug that is supposed to help induce milk supply. After being shown how to use a breast pump, I was able to achieve milk flow with the combination of both the pump and the drugs.

After the initial time spent in ICU, I was elated when Colin and Logan were healthy enough to come out of the incubators. After all the waiting, I could now invite family members to come to the hospital. It was during this visit, the nurse approached and said, "It's time to breastfeed. Let's pull the curtain for privacy; your Mom can stay and watch" and, as an afterthought, she added, "You don't mind, do you? She is, of course, your Mom." Inertly, I dreaded this, but what was I supposed to do? I couldn't very well say, "No, it's not okay." I started breastfeeding and, out of embarrassment, I must have turned many different shades of red. Do I need to remind you? - we didn't have a typical Mother/Daughter relationship, and the maternal bonding wasn't there.

On December 4, 1999, one more time, I was transferred back to Mackenzie Hospital by Air Ambulance. We were finally able to bring Colin and Logan home, and it would be a long-awaited, joyous celebration on Christmas day.

Logan, having cerebral palsy, was diagnosed with right-sided hemiplegia, a partial paralysis of one side of his body. We enlisted the help of the Infant Development Program to receive advice and support for Logan's disability. As well, since Colin and Logan were premature, we made scheduled yearly visits to B.C. Children's Hospital for their assessments.

Being new parents, we had a lot to learn, and a lot of sleepless nights were in store for us. Without family or friends, and not possessing the natural instinct, we managed to figure it out along the way with a few helpful tips from the nursing hotline. We didn't take anything for granted and enjoyed our hectic, busy lives.

We'd chuckle remembering the times. Colin and Logan were unwilling to do without their "Soothie," a pacifier given to us by the hospital. With the pacifiers getting worn out, we went and bought a different brand. The minute the pacifier reached their mouth, they both spat them out, crying in protest. They both wanted the Soothie they were used to, and nothing else would do. Desperate, we called the hospital and explained our situation. They laughed when we asked, "By any chance, can we buy some of your pacifiers?"

The first-time Colin and Logan had a treat, their first taste of ice cream. Noah held the cone as Logan took a lick, and then another until Noah thought he'd better stop, or else Logan would be sick. Every time Noah tried to take the ice cream away, Logan would scream in protest. We laughed so hard, and what were we to do? - We let him keep on licking. There was no stopping him! Sure enough, it would be Colin's turn next, and yet again the same.

Another time, taking them to Disneyland and watching in great pleasure as their eyes opened wide in wonderment and awe at the magic of the kingdom.

We still had our challenges and hardships, but we managed on our own. When Colin and Logan turned three years old, we decided to move back to the Lower Mainland, and be with family. We thought, "It was about time they knew their family, and maybe it would turn around."

With Logan's ongoing condition, we transferred to the Infant Development Program in Mission, B.C., and then to the Child Development Centre. At three-years-old, Logan and Colin had their unique language, just like Tess and me. Taking part in the Speech Therapy Program at the Child Development Centre, we were encouraged to learn sign language, a very useful tool to get children to develop speech.

One day at home, I was so focused on memorizing, practicing, and vocalizing the different hand signs, I didn't notice Colin and Logan imitating my every move. *This is going to be easier than I imagined,* I thought, laughing to myself. I couldn't believe the ease they had in learning sign language and, in a very brief time, they were talking.

In between preschool and starting work at a one-owner concrete testing firm in 2003, my schedule was full. A very flexible job, I was able to pick my hours and take Colin and Logan to work with me.

With kindergarten approaching, I had the option of starting Colin and Logan early at four years old or, waiting until they turned five. In 2004, I decided, "Why not enroll them early?" The first day of kindergarten was a very heartbreaking moment. Waiting outside for school to open, a few kids had already gathered and were lined up waiting for the bell to ring. Rambunctious, they played amongst themselves, with Logan trying to be a part of their activities. All his efforts went unheeded, and with a look of innocence he looked at me and asked, "Why does no one want to play with me?" It broke my heart that from this day on, Logan would have to contend with the cruelty of school, for being too slow, and physically not able to do activities as well as the other kids. He turned from a happy-go-lucky child to being shy, subdued, and quiet.

Imagine if you were "spaced out," and didn't have the ability to respond or remember. Locked in a world where you lost your cognitive and motor functions, and the only ability you had was a meaningless, repetitive behavior. All sense of rational and reasoning were gone as you lapsed into unconsciousness.

What I am explaining is a seizure that Logan would fall victim.

What is a seizure? In normal brain function, millions of tiny electrical charges pass from nerve cells in the brain to the rest of the body. A seizure occurs when the normal pattern is interrupted by sudden and unusually intense bursts of electrical energy.

In Grade 1 just before Christmas, Logan had his first seizure, and I did not have the insight or the knowledge to ascertain his condition. What started as a routine morning with me getting ready, Noah off to work, and Logan and Colin still in bed sleeping, would turn into a terrifying nightmare. Hearing a noise coming from Logan and Colin's bedroom, I went to investigate. Logan, laying on the top bunk, was sitting up, muttering, and pulling at his socks. At first, I thought he was in a deep state of sleepwalking. I asked him what he was doing, and his responses were completely out of sorts. Even after I helped remove his socks, his actions were the same. I told him to go back to sleep, but he didn't respond, and it was like he wasn't there. Worried he might fall out of bed, I helped him down and took him to the couch. Logan wasn't making any sense and, every time I asked him if he was okay, he answered with something completely bizarre that had nothing to do with what I asked. Paralyzing fear gripped me as I watched his progression worsen. Now, he was tilting his head up to the right, looking at the ceiling, and he held the stance. It was becoming more apparent that his ability to respond and his awareness were being affected. I started shouting his name in despair and tried to get him to snap out of the catatonic state he was experiencing. Helpless and, in a panic, I called Noah at work. With Noah's extensive first aid training and fire department experience, I figured he would know what to do. Sobbing, I shouted, "Something's wrong with Logan - I don't know what's going on." After giving Noah the lowdown, he said, "Hang up and phone 911 - I'm on my way home!" I did, and the ambulance was getting dispatched. Logan went into full arrest right outside Emergency and lapsed into unconsciousness. Running tests, the nurse went to draw blood and, Logan now conscious, but still in a catatonic state, went into a fit of rage. The nurse said, "I have to get a blood sample - can you hold him down? I can't believe how strong he is." All the while, Logan fought, scratching and biting to get away. I was so concentrated on Logan; I didn't realize Colin was standing nearby. He was watching in horror and, being so upset by what he saw he began to cry. I should have thought; feeling horrible, I told Noah to phone my Mom to see if she would come and pick Colin up.

After hours of examinations, blood work, and questions, they determined that Logan had suffered a seizure. To be safe, he was getting admitted to the hospital for a couple of days. We spent our Christmas at the hospital, and Logan was getting discharged the day after.

I had never let my Mom know about Logan having cerebral palsy, and didn't tell anyone, not at first. It was a decision made when he was born as I did not want him treated differently because of his disability. Maybe I was wrong, but I thought, *Colin and Logan will get treated as equals - no favorites here, not this time.* I wasn't about to gamble with Logan's emotions and have him endure the insecurities I had growing up; he would already have enough in which to cope. In the end, my Mom only knew about the seizures, and for the time being that is how it was left.

The second relapse happened just before summer break in Grade 1. Once more, in the morning, but now I knew what it was, and quickly called 911. This time, determining that Logan would have to go on medication to try and control the seizures.

Thirteen

In the summer of 2007, I began having migraine headaches so severe they lasted excruciating three full days straight. Besides the headaches, I would feel tired and didn't seem to have my usual energy. It seemed every three to four weeks the headaches returned, and medication of any sort did not relieve my symptoms. Iron pills and vitamins were treating the fatigue and exhaustion, and the doctor told me I was anemic and had a vitamin B12 deficiency. At first, the pills seemed to give me a little boost of energy, and helped with the tiredness but, after a few months, I wasn't getting any better. Feeling out of sorts and frustrated, I made repeated visits to Dr. Swift's office looking for answers and a solution. At the same time, since I was already there, and, for no particular reason, I asked him if he could check my neck gland. I said, "I'm not one to complain, but my left gland has swelled for quite some time. It used to be about two-thirds the size of a golf ball, and it slowly went down, but it won't go away." After examination, Dr. Swift dismissed it saying, "It's probably the result of a virus or the flu. Don't worry about it; it'll go down." I said, "Okay, but I haven't had the flu." To make a long story short, his answer to me was, "There is nothing more I can do for you."

For four years, I did my best to put up with it - what choice did I have? By 2010, my ability to concentrate and my memory were being affected. I decided to quit my job, take some time off and, figured with some rest; I'd feel better.

Noah and I moved to Edmonton, Alberta in 2011, for financial reasons. By November, still mindful of the fact that I wasn't feeling well and, knowing something was wrong, I went to Dr. John Dungone, my new family doctor. I recounted my previous discussions and history with Dr. Swift and complained of being very tired, having no energy, a lack of concentration, and my breathing was now labored. I insisted, "Something is wrong - I have never had any health concerns, and I can't understand why I'm having these symptoms. The only thing I'm taking is B12, and I go every two weeks for a shot - but it's not helping." He said, "You shouldn't be taking B12 every two weeks; it should only be given once a month." I said, "I know - I was on it every month, and it wasn't helping, so I decided to go every two weeks instead."

After thorough assessments and blood work, Dr. John said, "You're healthy; there's nothing wrong." Tired of the rigmarole and, unable to shake the feeling that something was wrong, I bombarded Dr. John for answers. At my wit's end, my frustration was now getting the better of me. He calmly replied, "We will keep going until we find something." One day, right out of the blue, I asked, "Could you check my gland?" and I pointed to the left side of my neck. I reminded him it had been swollen back in 2007 but had since gone down. Dr. John, after examining my neck said, "I don't see anything; it's probably nothing but, since we are checking everything, we may as well check this too." He really must have thought at this point that I was a hypochondriac, and I think he did this only to appease me. In March 2012, he sent me to Dr. Allan Erwin, a specialist in Otolaryngology. After performing a laryngoscopy, I went for an ultrasound, which showed cysts in my lymph node on the left side of my neck. He recommended that we obtain a tissue biopsy.

The biopsy results came back as malignant, and on May 24, 2012, the diagnosis was Non-Hodgkin's Lymphoma, Stage 3. Devastated by the news, I was in shock as I never dreamed I would have cancer at 53 years old! No one in my family had cancer, and I knew it wasn't hereditary. I said to Dr. Erwin, "That would explain why I'm so tired," and he replied, "Yes."

Lymphoma is a cancer of the lymph cells. The lymph cells are a type of blood cell that is known as white blood cells found in the blood and lymph nodes. As the cancer cells grow and multiply, the lymph nodes enlarge and form lumps. The cancer is detected as painless lumps in the neck, armpits or groin, and spreads to the other organs of the body.

He referred me to Dr. Reindeer, an Oncologist at the Cancer Clinic in Edmonton. Questioning her, I asked, "How did I get lymphoma?" and she replied, "There is no answer; no one knows what causes it." After further consultation, I asked, "Can't you take it out?" and she responded, "You're Stage 3 - if it had been

diagnosed at Stage 1 back in 2007, as you say, they could have done surgery but, since it has spread, surgery is not an option." Great - just my luck, I had been misdiagnosed!

After performing a CT scan, Dr. Reindeer reported that the lymphoma was evident in my neck and abdomen, therefore, a bone marrow aspirate, and needle core biopsy needed to eliminate the chances of cancer having spread. The procedure performed with the patient lying on their side, the skin cleansed, and a local anesthetic is injected to numb the area. An aspirate needle is first inserted through the skin using manual pressure and force until it abuts the bone. Then, with a twisting motion, the needle is advanced through the bone cortex (the hard outer layer of the bone), and into the marrow cavity. Once the needle is in the marrow cavity, a syringe is attached and used to aspirate (suck out) liquid bone marrow. A biopsy is then performed using a different, larger trephine needle; inserting and anchoring into the bone cortex to obtain a solid piece of bone marrow.

At my first appointment, the doctor was unable to perform the procedure successfully. After repeated attempts, he was not able to insert the needle into the desired location and took his frustration out on me. Treating me like a "slab of meat," he pushed me harshly to reposition me, and said, "Stop moving!" I did not appreciate his curt manner and retorted, "I'm not moving - I'm doing what you said exactly!" Failing again, he had no choice but to call in Dr. Dave, the head of surgery, for advice. Having exhausted the maximum dosage of the anesthetic, I had to make another appointment. This time, it would be Dr. Dave who performed the procedure. Boy, talk about night and day - Dr. Dave had a bedside manner! A friendly, senior man of around 60 years of age, he made small talk to put me at ease. He told of his upbringing and being raised on a farm. He said, "Who would have thought a farm boy is turning out to be a doctor?!" From the onset, he calmly explained his every step and stated, "It isn't difficult; if you feel any pain or discomfort, just let me know. All it means is I've come too close to the nerve and need to reposition the needle." As if in confirmation, pain shot down my leg, and telling Dr. Dave, he repositioned the needle; it was so simple, and the procedure was over on the first try. Finishing up, Dr. Dave said, "Don't get up yet - I'll be right back." Coming back into the room, he handed me an 8 x 10 print and said, "I want you to have this. I'm into photography in my spare time, and I captured this photo of a loon mid-flight landing in a marshy lake in the backcountry." I commented on how good it was and felt honored he would even think about giving it to me. Before I left, as an afterthought, I asked the nurse, "Can you request Dr. Dave to sign this - he has to autograph it!" The results of my bone marrow showed no evidence of malignant lymphoma detected.

The determination was to take the "Wait and See" approach since the lymph nodes were not increasing in size. By August 2012, I was sent for another biopsy, this time to my left groin as it had spread. Once again, Dr. Reindeer indicated that it would be in my best interest not to proceed with chemotherapy as I wasn't experiencing any B symptoms, and there had been some reduction in the size of some of the lymph nodes.

Finding out about my cancer hit us hard. It was difficult living with the thought that the lymphoma could progress at any time, and I could die. Noah and I then made the decision to move back to B.C., - that way, if I needed help, my family would be there. In June 2013, we moved back to Surrey, B.C., and I resumed my treatment in August at the BC Cancer Agency next to Surrey Memorial Hospital. Dr.

Richardson would now be my Oncologist.

Appointments were scheduled every three months, and I had the usual tests: blood work, exams, and CT scans. Multiple lymph nodes were evident in my neck, abdomen, and groin. I am facing the scary realization that the lymphoma has spread throughout my body. As the lymph nodes increased in size, I started having bladder control problems. I told Dr. Richardson, "I can't hold my bladder, and I constantly have to go." With that, he responded, "I think we should go ahead with chemotherapy, especially since it's pushing on your bladder." In April 2014, I started chemotherapy treatment.

At the onset, it was Noah who came with me to the hospital. Six hours initially, and about four hours of treatment from then on. Let alone nausea, vomiting, the metal taste in my mouth; I was having trouble eating and sleeping. The worst part was, it was physically draining. Quite literally, I had nothing left and was in excruciating pain. It was at this point I knew it could go either way. I did not have the strength to fight. The first couple of treatments I was in such intense pain and would go home, take a sleeping pill, and go to bed; Childbirth was a piece of cake compared to this. It felt like my insides were being bombarded with missiles constantly taking aim, and steadily attacking different parts of my body; this was target practice, and I was the target! Then, my hair fell out, and not just a couple of strands here and there. I was continually pulling chunks of hair out and had no choice but to go and buy a wig. Shaving my head was not easy as I thought, *boy if I wasn't insecure before, I sure am now! Oh well, I can't do anything about it now - I have bigger problems to worry about.*

I went every three weeks for chemotherapy, a duration of nine cycles of a drug treatment called CVPR, abbreviated in short, that included five cancer-fighting drugs. In December 2014, I would continue undergoing "maintenance" chemotherapy for another two years, and go every three months unless, of course, something changed. There would be a steady array of cat scans and blood work to monitor my progress. Then, receiving a phone call from Dr. Richardson, informing me, "Reviewing your reports from Edmonton, I noticed you have cystic nodules in your thyroid. One is borderline; it's 1.5 cm in size. Let's do an ultrasound and biopsy." At least here, the results turned out favorably, and they were benign.

The lymph nodes have decreased in size, but I am still exhausted, tired, have no energy, strength or concentration. In my ears, I have a constant ringing now, and it never goes away. My bladder remains a problem. My short-term memory has been affected, and I have to write things down now as I am unable to retain them. I found watching a program one day, there is such a condition for the memory loss - it's called Chemo Brain. My hands and feet went numb, which improved when the doctor decreased the amount of medication. I've put on weight, am dizzy and lightheaded, my stomach swelled most of the time, and I deal with steady pain. I have come down with neuropathy, another side effect of chemotherapy, which will eventually get better. I am unable to work, and with it comes the isolation. My inability to concentrate and the fatigue have slowed my reflexes, which has impacted my ability to drive. I don't drive unless I have to as I get too stressed out.

Chemotherapy puts a toll on your body and your defenses. You can only take so much, but then I think, "Have to do it, and this is the only treatment that can help - so I can't stop now." I'm just waiting for the day when I can feel well and return to my life.

Dealing with cancer threw me for a loop, especially after realizing the extremity of my condition, and what was to come. I assumed, "Okay I've got cancer - I'll go for chemo, and I'll be better." Wow was I wrong! I have always been strong, had the inner strength to cope, but the journey had just begun. I honestly thought and, expected, my family to be there for me. Not once, have I been one to ask for help as I never wanted to put anyone out but, this time, I really would have welcomed the assistance and support. Full of pride and, never one to complain, I wasn't forthright in asking for help. It was a devastating blow to realize that after everything I'd done for everyone else, without waiting to be asked, no one was there – unless, of course, you think a phone call is enough; that is what I got. Overcome with an overwhelming sense of feeling completely alone and deeply hurt was when the soul searching began.

Noah and I handled things on our own, and no offer to help ever came. No one thought, "I'll just drop in, see if she needs a hand or go up to the hospital. There must be something I can do." My outlook still high, I held on to the glimmer of hope that family would eventually come around. Again, using common sense, *Okay, it's not a good time,* I thought. *I'll give them a chance; I'll wait.* I even went as far as to fly to Montreal in 2014, going in between chemotherapy treatments to visit my Mom and Helen. I had to see them one more time as it might be the last time.

I waited a year, and nothing changed. By this point, I had lost all patience - the wait was over, enough being enough, and I blew up! I would be on my deathbed before anyone shows up. Family is supposed to be there for you. I was adamant in my thinking. I was curtly told, "we can't read your mind!"

Going through cancer opens your eyes. Not only do you review your life, but you also hope that acknowledgment was given, and told you do mean something. At the very least, I thought someone would come over, and just let me talk. Not to be melodramatic, but I thought my family would want to spend time with me not knowing when, or if, I was going to die.

I was concerned that if something did happen, I would have someone I could rely on, and tell my final wishes. It didn't happen though, and I was still alone. I couldn't talk to Noah; I didn't wish to burden him any further as he had enough on his plate too. Every other time in my life, I had the inner strength to cope and had fight left in me to do it by myself. This time, I am drained - mentally and physically, it was taking its toll, and I had no strength left. When I thought, I couldn't feel worse, it got worse - and then a whole lot worse. It would have been nice to have some help or support, not for the sake of chores, but only to come over just once to let me know I count. My role has always been the "listener," and I am the "peacemaker" for everyone around - listening to their problems, and so I thought that maybe I could talk this time. Not so, it seemed; it hadn't changed.

My problem has always been when I'm sick; I don't look sick. No one realizes how I am feeling, and just assumes because I look good, I must be fine. I think no one can truly understand unless someone has gone through it. So many times, I've said, "I'm tired," and my only reply is, "Oh, me too!" Starting from the moment I get up, to the time I go to bed, I am always tired. I continue to block it out as I have Colin and Logan to look after. Every once in a while, I would think, "God, it would be nice just for a day not to be tired, have the energy I used to have, and be able to do the things I used to do." That is the problem with cancer - there is never a break in-between, you can't re-energize, and every day you are faced with not feeling well.

It hit me one day - an epiphany! I don't need confirmation of my life and was struck with the knowledge it comes from within. I know what I have done, I can feel proud of who I am, and what I've done! It was a turning point - it finally clicked, made sense, and at last, I felt it from within.

Now though, I can't keep my emotions in check, and under control. I speak up, not out of spite but, for the first time, to stick up for myself, to have a say, and to have a voice. I became vocal, a far cry from keeping quiet to try and please in the hopes of being accepted and liked.

The last time anyone got together was six years ago, for Victor's, my stepfather's funeral. The disbelief and sadness sweep in, and the hurt I feel sinks in knowing that no one cares enough. Bottom line, it's a matter of convenience, isn't it? No one wants to put in the effort to go out of their way. I expected maybe one or two of my family members not to be there, but not all of them!

I was the first to admit that I could have handled it differently, but I still wasn't about to take back what I said. I brought up the many times I helped without being asked. It wasn't to brag or to compare, but only to say, "I don't deserve this - I've been there for you, so why can't you be there for me?" Even that, was taken the wrong way, and everyone went on the defensive - the one comment made, "I'm sick and tired of hearing what you've done."

I thought that now they would understand, and maybe we could talk. At the very least, it would be a start. The visits came sporadically, a couple of times a year - and only out of necessity, to hear about their problems. I would listen as they filled me in on their exciting get-a-way holidays, and shopping bonanzas - their preference was to go out, enjoy their free time, and do what they wanted instead of being cooped up with me. Their lives were normal, and without the support, it was as if they were blatantly throwing it up in my face. Did they not understand, with cancer, I am unable to do this right now, and it just invokes more inadequacies, insecurities, and frustrations on my part? I couldn't help but feel I was on the bottom of the totem pole, and their behavior implied, that they would come over only when they had nothing better to do. The rejection hit tantamount proportions when my Mom booked a flight to come out and, the day before she was to arrive, she canceled her flight, unsure of whether or not she should come. If I had to force her or of she needed to really think about it, then it's not worth the trouble. Don't let me put you out. The day after her canceled flight, my mom called to let me know that she was thankful that she had canceled the trip as Helen had rescued a litter of puppies and brought them home, so she wouldn't have looked after her dog, Cocoa. Cocoa was my Mom's dog, and after Victor's passing, it was she who filled the void by becoming my mother's sole companion.

Not one of them realizes that cancer does not give you a break, and it is a struggle every day. I have not had one good day since I started, and do not have the luxury or freedom to be able just to get up and go. At the very least, I know where I stand, and I'm not so gullible now. The phone calls are more of a chore, something extra I need to contend with as now it feels like a slap in the face. The worst part is, they all think they're supporting me - far from it. It's a painful reminder that I am still alone, and, with all their good intentions, I manage on my own.

My sister said to me once, "I know what you're going through."

Angered by her thoughtlessness, I retorted, "How would you know? Do you have cancer?! Have I told you what my symptoms are, or have you seen what I suffer through?! Have you even gone to the Cancer Centre?" Then I realized that they have no idea. They can't pretend like you know what I'm going through – it was insulting!

Even worse, are the "attention grabbers" who thrive on attention, and think they are far worse off than anyone else. They overreact to the slightest concern with their health, and think they are entitled to preferential treatment. With my patience borderline, it is bothersome and annoying.

It's funny, I've received more offers to help by Ivy, a woman my husband knows at work. I thought, "It takes a total stranger to show more concern and willingness to help than my family."

I was searching for the "Leave It to Beaver" type of family. Perhaps it's fantasy; do families like that even exist or, is it just a pipe dream? Then I turn around and take in the family unity I see all around me. Other families. I realize this is how it should be and, again, I see the good. If you alone have to try so hard to resolve the conflict, is it worth resolving? Is it worth the effort if nobody else is willing to make the effort to meet you?

My cancer diagnosis and treatment precipitated my need to reflect on my life. I felt I was running out of time, made the decision to write this book and, in so doing, wanted answers from my Mom. For the first time, I needed to question her, and ask her why she made the choices that she did. I was completely out of my comfort zone, but thought this would be only time that we could have this talk. Showing my vulnerable side, I voiced my feelings of rejection and insecurity, and my Mom could not comprehend what I was trying so hard for her to grasp. All these years, her grief and loss over Melanie had stayed in the forefront - my pain was overshadowed, forgotten about, and I was second best. I never expected her to dismiss Melanie - her suicide, but I only wanted to have some consolation that she cared about me also - Wasn't I sexually abused too?"

I broached the topic of why she had "kicked" Tess and me out of the house at sixteen. Her response was, "I didn't kick you out - I helped you." Incredulously, I stammered, "What?! How did you help? You kicked us out!" She said, "With all the fighting going on, I thought you were old enough or, would be soon, to get out on your own." I replied, "Well okay, but why me? I wasn't fighting - I wasn't doing anything wrong, so why did I have to leave?" She cattily remarked, "Would you have preferred I kept you at home, so Dad could keep abusing you?!" Flabbergasted, I couldn't even answer; this had gone beyond the point of no return and was uncalled for. I thought, "You didn't even know about Dad, so how can you even say that?!" Still wanting answers, I collected myself and continued the arduous questions. Calmly, I asked, "After you found out about Dad, why did you take him back?" She said, "I had Helen to look after, and by this time you and Tess were out of the house. I didn't think he would touch Helen, his daughter." The way I saw it, I was kicked out to get rid of the conflict at home, and it came down to a matter of convenience. What better way, than to kill two birds with one stone, and get rid of both of us at once?

She could not fathom it and thought instead that I was accusing and placing blame. How wrong she was; I only wanted answers, and to try and make her understand how inadequate I felt. I had dealt with the past, never judged, and I just wanted someone to notice; be validated. She shrugged it off by saying, "I'm sorry, I don't know what you want from me," and ended by stating, "I think you had a pretty good childhood other than the abuse" - apparently, the tendency to, once again, assume it was trivial. Then I reflect, "Is it me?" Deep in thought, I played it over and over again in my head - "It's over, done, so what is it I'm looking for?" The answer came, "Remorse - she can't show remorse, not for me anyway." Her excuse - "I didn't know." All I wanted was for her to give me some credit, and to realize that I got through it on my own - with no help from anyone. As if it couldn't get any worse, she asked, "Why didn't you tell me? - then Melanie would still be alive." Talk about plunging a knife into my soul, and with it, I thought, "Okay, now I get it. You're blaming me." Vehemently, I replied, "It wasn't just me - no one told you!"

Her words invoked a deep sense of sadness, hurt, and rejection. It left me feeling like I should have been the one to have committed suicide, that way, the abuse would not have continued, it would have stopped with me, and Melanie would still be alive. Then maybe, I would have been given her undying love - instead of her minimizing my abuse.

I can only sum up, "I was invisible for most of my childhood." To explain, I did not cause trouble, certainly did not talk, and did what I was told to do. I stayed in the background – therefore, I was out of sight, and out of mind. For the most part, left to my defenses - my Mom, busy dealing with the turmoil, my Dad's drinking, his affairs, the fighting, problems at school, the workings of her daily life, Melanie's suicide and then, to top it all off, the sexual abuse. I realized a lot of my childhood memories I discussed with her she hadn't even been aware. Appearances alone, she only saw what was on the surface, and it never went deeper than that. It was quite a shock for both of us to realize how very little she knew of me, and I had been lumped together as one with Tess.

After some time, my Mom said, "I don't like you saying I kicked you out. I'd rather you said you moved out." I replied, "You kicked us out!" and she said, "No, I helped you, and I got you an apartment." In response, I answered, "I had no choice, no say – you did not ask ... that means if you look it up, I was kicked out, and it wasn't an agreement!" Besides the fact, we were only 16 years old.

There was no resolution, and what I hoped would be a turning point, a coming together, ended up being the biggest mistake ever. The regret sunk in as I thought, "I should have known better."

My Mom does not like conflict and, unable to deal with it, she will do her best to avoid it. Besides the fact, she has Shingles and has lived with it now for about four years. She's getting on, twenty years older than me, and my timing couldn't have been worse. Though it was out of my control, and with cancer, I had no recourse – it has to happen. I thought, "Before one of us dies, we need to clear the air." Besides, it wouldn't have mattered at what point I had brought it up; she had her views, and I had mine. My intentions were good, and at the very least I had some answers now. For her sake as well as mine, we needed to have this talk. I realize my Mom and I will never see "eye to eye" - our viewpoints are not the same, but at least I tried. Maybe there is too much excess baggage with me that she would rather forget, and on a subconscious level, I am still paying the price.

Writing this book, I thought, for the most part, I would receive encouragement – instead, a backlash implying I had no right, it was best to leave it in the past, and not write about Melanie or my childhood. I couldn't believe it! Did they not know I needed to do this for myself, and it was important to me?

Two years now, and I'm fed up. I'm tired of the rejection, the excuses, the misunderstandings, and not getting any help. I'm tired of cancer, not feeling good, not looking good, having no holidays, not being able to work, and the financial burden.

In one word, I miss the normalcy of my life.

Up to this point, I was coping, and, in the back of my mind, I was still waiting, holding out that it would change. I did not push, and thought, "If I mean anything, if I'm important enough, my family will come around." Not so it seems - I'm not a priority and with it, the hurt and anger settled in. The realization came crashing down - the overwhelming pain, and the betrayal that all my efforts were in vain. My parting words were, "Boy, you all had me fooled!" Once more, I was "invisible," and didn't count.

They all thought I was having "issues" in dealing with the past, but that wasn't it at all - it was the present which concerned me. I was hoping once and for all the family unity, the closeness would finally be there, and cancer would bring us more close. The anger didn't arise because of my "issues!" (I am sarcastic here) - It came from the frustration that, no matter what I did, our family wasn't close. It was shrugged off by saying, "This is how our family is." No one wanted to talk or understand what it was I was asking them. All it would have taken were a few words of encouragement by simply saying, "Wow, I give you credit; I don't know how you can cope, and I hope you know how much you mean to me." Instead, thought that I was being resentful, making a big deal out of nothing, and expecting too much. I should have known not to hope for anything different.

Being forthright in expressing my feelings made everyone

uncomfortable and awkward. They were all too eager to dismiss it without anything in return. It's discouraging as I know I have done nothing to deserve this. Ironic, my Dad has received better treatment than me. Even after my Mom and Dad got divorced, and he remarried, Helen and Billy both kept in contact with him. It wasn't until after the court case that they both realized, "My God, maybe there's some truth to this," and stopped all contact with him.

My foundation was shaken to the inner core - my sense of belonging, and acceptance wasn't there. I did not receive any special treatment, and it was no different than before. Foregone conclusion, it is what it is. You know the saying, "You can lead a horse to water, but you can't make it drink." The loss, the pain, is from knowing that I cannot change what is. I have come to accept that I can only change myself.

Ever hear the saying, "Throw the dog a bone?" Well, that is what I feel. I thought, "I've done nothing to deserve this and, still in utter disbelief and shock, my patience finally ran out. Inundated with their indifference, their excuses, and every attempt at reconciliation made me feel minuscule, inferior for even suggesting that they should be here. Well, I'm not begging anymore - I am not a charity case, and I'm done asking. My self-esteem and self-confidence at an all-time low, and my emotional state wreaking havoc, it was becoming more detrimental to my health. I thought, "This will kill me faster than cancer ever will." With the stress being the deciding factor, my self-preservation kicked in, and I made a choice. To stay focused and, get better, for my well-being I decided to stop contact for a while. I thought, "For everyone's benefit, maybe it's time to take a break, let everyone clear their head, and have some space."

I must say, if I hear "I love you" one more time, I'm going to scream! They're only words - nice and easy, isn't it? The not talking lasted only a month when the phone calls resumed.

It turns out in the month I didn't talk to my Mom, she had sold her house in Montreal, and Cocoa died quite unexpectedly of cancer.

I thought Cocoa dying from cancer would make her understand my anxiety, my need to spend time together ... I, too, have cancer.

What is normally no big deal, is a big deal when you have cancer. I'm not the easiest person to get along with right now; I'm not jovial and much too serious right now – Excuse me! The simple, plain truth is my outlook would be a whole lot better if a show of support given when I need it. I'm not demanding, am very easy going, don't expect much, and let a lot slide without complaint.

I have never been one to hurl insults, and my belief is, "If I haven't got anything good to say, I don't say it at all." I'm not out to hurt anyone. My downfall is I haven't spoken up and objected to the assumptions or judgments. That is where I've changed. Now, I am outspoken and, if something upsets me, I vocalize it. I don't keep it buried anymore.

To make matters worse, I've had to contend with the derogatory comments, as I call it the "digs," about not only my physical appearance but my integrity.

Besides my family, I've had comments made that were criticizing and are uncalled.

Like the time my hair fell out and, wearing a knitted hat one day, a woman drove by and shouted out, "Try wearing a baseball cap!" Another time, at chemotherapy, a patient's husband asked, "What are you in here for?" I replied, "Lymphoma; I come every three weeks," and he remarked, "Aren't you lucky - we have to come every week!"

More so, my family. The first time my sister saw me wearing a wig, her immediate reaction was to laugh, which I didn't find appropriate or appreciate. I thought, "Thanks for the encouragement." The criticisms about my physical appearance continued with my gray hair (after it grew back), the dark circles under my eyes, the weight gain caused by chemotherapy, and the list went on. I thought to myself, "How can you be so insensitive? - Give me a break. I've got cancer - what's your excuse? You're one to talk." That is the difference; I would never dream of saying anything hurtful, preferring instead to pay a compliment or give an encouraging word.

My character and integrity then came into question. I spend my spare time drawing, sculpting, carving, and doing photography. It wasn't professional by any means, but I had some natural talent. Even with this, the praise wasn't forthcoming; derogatory remarks - "It's good, but ...," and saying I didn't have a maternal instinct since I didn't know how to put on a diaper the very first time, just to name a few. Implying I was overprotective since I didn't give Colin and Logan enough freedom. My answer, "Would it have been better if I let them walk the streets, do drugs, drink, and drop out of school?!"

The "digs" have been a constant throughout my life, and the remarks have implanted self-doubt and inadequacy. Maybe, I'm overly sensitive, but the negative comments have piled up, and it finally dawned on me, I put up with a lot of negativity. I can take criticism, but sometimes it would be nice to hear something positive to counteract the negative.

Resigned, I thought, "It doesn't matter what I do, and I'm done trying to prove myself. I could have given an 110%, and it would not have been enough - the "insults" would still have come." It was a hard pill to swallow, and right now I'm drained. I don't want to hear anymore, and thought, "Doesn't anyone have anything good to say?!" My favorite word now is "whatever," think what you will - I'm just glad to be alive! Words can hurt even if your intentions are good. People need to think before they speak; a kind word goes a whole lot further.

The smallest chore is an effort, and so many times I would hold myself back from collapsing, breaking down, and crying out in pure exhaustion. I would force myself to block it out and, mentally taking note, I would think, "You have no choice, you have to do it." Multitasking is out, and now I take it one step at a time at a much slower pace.

If it weren't for cancer, I probably would not have reacted in earnest. Too much all at once and with very little resistance, everything sets me off. Having cancer, I thought, "I must matter a little bit." Then as time passed, I pondered, "It's not just me - does anyone think about Noah, Colin, and Logan, and how it's affecting them? Do they not realize they, too, are having a difficult time, and maybe they could use a helping hand as well?"

A comment made by a counselor at the initial cancer group session, "Don't get angry with family members; sometimes, they are unsure of what to do to help. Understand they too are at a loss," and then I laugh. Not in my case - no one offered to help, and no one wanted to put forth the effort.

Looking at the bigger picture, I now take the attitude, "To each his own," and maybe that's okay because I cannot hold a grudge, turn bitter, and throw all the years away. On the same hand, though, I will not fall back into the trap - into my old ways, trying to please, and blaming myself. I have come too far, and will not take on the negative innuendos, the "insults" as I call them, and project them back onto me. I have to keep reminding myself - I have done nothing to deserve this, I feel good about what I've done, and the responsibility lies with them as well. At the very least I was able to voice my feelings even if not returned. I keep on asking the question, "What is so hard to understand?"

After this, I happened by chance upon an article called, "Loyalty Vs. Blind Loyalty in Families," written by Mary Jane Hurley Brant, a practicing Human Relations Counselor and Certified Group Psychotherapist and Grief Specialist. Quoting from her, "Loyalty is essential for genuine family solidarity, but blind loyalty leads to family dysfunction."

I realized there had been no lines of open communication and, as a result, I repressed my emotions. I took on the role of peacemaker to gain approval, love, and acceptance. I blindly followed, adapted to the dysfunction, and was obedient in my efforts not to upset or anger anyone. With the onset of cancer, I challenged our family views and spoke out for the first time against the dysfunction. Ill-equipped to suppress my feelings of hurt and rejection substantiated by the lack of support has met me with denial and disapproval.

One thing I know for certain is, I give credit where it's due, and right now it happens to be Noah; he is the one who is there for me.

The worst part of cancer is not knowing what comes next; the uncertainty is always looming over your head. The unknown isn't like getting surgery - you get the operation, you are fixed, and get better – No, even if you go into remission, a term doctors don't like to use the cancer is always lurking waiting to come back. I try not to think of this anymore, take it one day at a time, and leave it in God's hands. I'm not giving up and am more determined than ever to do it on my own. Noah, unfortunately, has taken the brunt of all my frustrations, depression, upsets, and worries. It is Noah who helps, and not to forget Logan and Colin, who are my inspiration too.

Cancer has brought Noah and me even closer if that is indeed possible. We talk and express our feelings on a much deeper level now whereas, before, it didn't seem to be an issue.

I have never been one for taking statistics too seriously. My rule of thumb is, "What will be ... will be." If I had listened to the statistics, I would have given up, and never had children. So now, I think the same. Everyone dies, and you will only die when it is your time.

Once, when I was going for chemotherapy, another patient, a man around sixty-five years old, whispered, "This is the shits isn't it?" My response was, "Yes, but you get through it." He didn't argue, nodded, and after thinking about it said, "Yeah, I guess you have a point."

I don't feel sorry for myself. From the moment I entered the Chemotherapy Room; I came to the daunting realization that I was only one out of many with cancer - each person with a different type of cancer, each in different stages of treatment, and each with varying degrees of treatment. At this point, none better or worse for each person had their struggle. For that is what cancer is; it is a fight for life - wouldn't be here otherwise.

Fourteen

Two and a half years of chemotherapy and I'm at the final stage. I am still filled with anxiety not knowing what the future holds, but I have finally found my peace of mind. Cancer has given me a chance, the time to reflect on my life, and the opportunity to fulfill and correct any misgivings before I die. When that will be, who knows? – It could be a year or ten years from now. Either way, I have come to terms with it; I've done the best I can, and I'm all right.

As for my family, I have let go of the anger brought on by the hurt. It is futile, and I will not let the petty differences get in the way. In the end, it's not so important who is right and who is wrong. The fact remains, "You will miss them when they're gone," and it will only be the loss that you have left to hold.

It has opened the door to remember the special moments that I had forgotten about and, with each memory, it brings a smile:

As a toddler, riding my bike for the very first time without the training wheels. As I hesitantly wobbled back and forth, I gathered speed and was filled with immense pleasure as I kept my balance and second nature took over.

The excitement of going to the corner store with coins in hand to buy penny candy. Not only was I thrilled about the candy, but this was the first time I had been given money, even though it was only a few cents in change.

The first time I'd ever been in a rowboat and my Grandfather paddled us out around the lake. The time spent bonding with my Grandfather as the quiet solitude was interrupted only by the noise of the gentle ripples of the oars cutting through the water.

The exhilaration and wonderment at taking my first flight in a small light aircraft. My Uncle Barry had his private pilot's license, and we soared over Vancouver and across the Lower Mainland. How very different it looked from the vantage point of a plane.

My Grandmother when moving back from Australia brought us presents - an authentic stuffed koala bear and a kangaroo pouch.

The first time I stood at the top of the stairs and had the crazy notion that if I jumped, I could fly. The exhilaration as I catapulted, and only managed to stumble at the remaining last three steps before I crashed into the door.

The baking my Mom did, especially at Christmas time. The treats, batch after batch and placed in the freezer to keep. All of us would sneak down, and take some as we couldn't resist the temptation, nor could we wait.

Christmas presents hidden in the closet and, as soon as my Mom and Dad went out, we would pull out bag after bag of unwrapped gifts to find what each one of us had got.

The time with Ricky, Melanie's boyfriend, when we stayed up all night talking in the car. The peacefulness and quiet solitude as we watched the beauty of the early morning sunrise.

The first time I drove my car after getting my driver's license, and the thrill of having the freedom to drive, blare the music, and go wherever I chose.

The first time going to the beach in White Rock and, with the tide going out, Noah and I ventured further out among the gentle tidal waves. Confidently, I jumped into the cool refreshing water unaware my tube top had slipped down as soon as I sprung up. Noah is hurriedly shouting, "Pull your top up!" and thankfully, we were out far enough so no one else could see.

The time Noah and I were driving home, and the song, "Nine to Five," by Dolly Parton played over the radio. Both of us singing loudly in abandonment along with the music, and we couldn't contain our laughter when other drivers stared at us thinking we were insane.

Walking Logan and Colin to a school playground, and once we got to the parking lot gate, I said, "You better duck." Not knowing the phrase, they both asked, "Where?" and stood to look for the duck.

These are only a few of the special times, and I hold them tightly.

We all think we are invincible and have all the time in the world. Then it's too late, and all you have left are memories. That is why I choose to remember the good and, with the good, comes forgiveness. A time to reflect, to let go of the anger, and accept what is. I know I can only change myself and do the best I can.

Another chapter has just unfolded, and it is January 2017. My Mom diagnosed with an Aortic Aneurysm. The aorta is the largest artery in the body and runs all the way from the heart to the lower body. An aneurysm balloons out of an artery wall, a bit like what happens at a weak spot in an inner tube. She will need constant monitoring as it is still small. Her diagnosis is not good as, if it were to rupture, she will more than likely die and, if it increases in size, surgery will be extremely risky and dangerous, especially at her age.

The timing couldn't have come at a more inopportune moment and, with it, the realization that time has run out - the loss of not having a better relationship and, my regret is, that no matter how hard I tried, we could never get on the same page. We are two completely different people - talk about yin and yang. Our personalities, our likes, our lifestyle, and our viewpoints are not the same. Sometimes, even that is beyond your control, whatever the reason.

I said to my Mom one day, "You love me, but you don't like me."

I am facing another deep sense of loss for what could have been, how it could have been, and it is with sadness that I am unable to make her understand that all I wanted was to be loved and accepted. Even with all our differences, I still love her and will miss her deeply when she's gone.

My Mom is the matriarch of our family, she has been the mainstay, and it is her position that binds our family together. It seems she is the one, the common ground. Unfortunately, when she dies, so too, will the ties of our family unit. The need or desire to stay in touch will not be there on anyone's part. A long time in the making ... it was our upbringing that brought about the disconnect. Too many unresolved and painful memories to ignore, and then also, too much time has passed.

I have heard the stories of my Mom's childhood, her struggles, and the hardships she endured. That is why I will not judge her decisions and her choices. Do I agree with them? - No, but I can better understand her actions, and will not hold ill will. It is not in my makeup to be vindictive and hold a grudge, and I have never done so.

I have come to understand over the last three years, that cancer has changed my life, and my outlook. I am not so concerned with trying to please, to be accepted or to prove myself. Now, I figure if people don't like me for who I am, it's their loss. I like who I am, and my priority is to look ahead. I will pay it forward and will continue in my efforts to make the most out of my life.

Once again, the hurt is a constant, and it keeps rearing its ugly head. I continue to make excuses for everyone by trying to justify their actions to lessen the pain. I have got to stop doing that! Bottom line - there is no excuse. With it, comes a certain stubbornness, and I will not partake in or agree with their notion that they all think they are there for me. I will not allow them to take the credit, not this time.

Out of this whole experience, I have gained much more insight, have found myself, and for that, I am eternally grateful. Compounded, in the last three years, I have experienced a magnitude of emotions, realizations, and triumphs.

One deciding factor - I cannot change what is, but I have changed myself. In some respects, it's a release - a release of the burden, the insecurities, and the self-doubt that I'm not worthy enough. I can stop punishing myself and try to prove myself, to have someone like me. I am healing and with it comes a deeper awareness of my path. Most of all, it has set me free. I cannot control everyone else and can only control myself. They, like me, must find their way, and in their time, they will. So now I say, "Thank you, cancer - you have brought about my rebirth!"

Fifteen

Rarely do I dream so when I do, I take notice. Looking back, I realize there were many times I would experience the spiritual and, not thinking too much of it, would shrug it off. When I was younger, I would often drift into sleep, and have the sensation of going down a tunnel at full speed. There was no physical connection or body, and it felt like I was floating. It was a common occurrence, and each time I would be jolted back awake.

For years, I had this one particular dream, and it was so real, vivid, and crystal clear. This dream was always the same, but every time it would play out a step further. I am a little girl around six years old, and I am with my father, mother, and younger sister. My sister and I both have long blonde hair and are wearing dainty, white dresses suited to the era of the early 1800s. We are traveling by wagon train on a dirt shrouded trail leading through a dense forest. We had come to a stop, and I jumped off to run and play. My younger sister was not as quick, and she was still trying to get off the back of the wagon. A little distance away from the wagon, I was stricken with fear as, out of nowhere, a pack of wolves emerged. Growling and snarling, they were menacing. Stalking and descending towards me, I abruptly turned to run, terrified. At the same time, I screamed and shouted at my sister to stay where she was. As the wolves pounced, they savagely attacked, and viciously ripped me apart. At the moment of my impending death, I would jerk awake. I eventually stopped having this recurring dream.

I had woken up very late one night to the darkness and steady rhythmic, muffled sounds of everyone sleeping upstairs. Discernible in the stillness of the night I could hear a constant hubbub of conversation and laughter drifting up from the living room downstairs. It sounded like a social gathering, a party of such, but I couldn't make it out, what they were saying even though the clamor and bustle of conversation were loud. Confused, I crept down the stairs thinking, "I didn't know Mom and Dad were having a party tonight - they hadn't said anything." To my amazement, I found it dark, the lights were off, and it was silent. No one was up, and everyone was in bed sleeping.

Another time, I rounded the corner into the living room and noticed the rocking chair swaying back and forth, slowly coming to a stop. The thing was, no one was there! These occurrences would happen when I lived on Sprott Street, and nothing more would happen until I knew Noah.

When I first met Noah, he was taking a trip to Florida, and I was saying goodbye. We were standing at Camille's back door, and I was quite upset as I figured by the time Noah came back, he would have forgotten all about me. We were hugging and kissing and, suddenly, I felt a hand squeeze my shoulder from behind. It was a gentle and comforting touch as if reassuring me and telling me it would be okay. At first, I thought it was Noah but, when I looked down, he was wrapping his arms around my waist. "That's odd," I thought, trying to sort out what had just happened. I honestly couldn't say how, but instinctively I knew it was Noah's Dad, even though I had never met him.

I always questioned these experiences, looking for a rational explanation but, unable to come up with a logical or reasonable answer, I would continue to brush them off.

One time in Vancouver, during a reading, the medium started by saying, "You have a father figure here. I don't feel it's your father; he's on your husband's side." I said, "Yes, he's up there in the corner of the room," and I pointed to the ceiling. Needless to say, his mouth dropped open as he wasn't expecting this response. I had the ability to see him in my mind. The only way of explaining this is, "Imagine yourself looking at a photograph - you study it for a while and then place it away. Bring the photo back into your thoughts, and with it, you will have a clear image of what you saw." Like a memory playing out in your head or a movie reel playing back.

Many times, Noah's Dad has made himself known, not only to me but Noah as well. It's quite funny, Noah is the logical one, and is more of a skeptic.

The studio apartment we rented in New Westminster was a place we both experienced an undeniable spiritual event. We were sitting on the edge of our bed, talking, and out of nowhere, an orb materialized in front of us, shooting straight towards us. We both
broke apart as this orb traveled right between us and then vanished. Stunned, I looked at Noah and asked, "Did you see that?" We sat visibly shaking as we could not fathom or register what we had just witnessed.

I even have a photograph of a ghost. We were living at Camille's, and I was in the driveway snapping pictures of Noah working on an old Ford pickup truck he just bought. When I developed the film, I noticed in one of the photographs a figure of a young boy standing beside Noah. The image of the young boy was translucent and, I knew the day I took the photo, Noah and I were the only ones in the driveway.

Astral projection or travel denotes the astral body leaving the physical body to travel in an astral plane. This one morning, my mother-in-law, Camille, spoke of an incident that left her worried, and a little upset. During a phone conversation with her daughter, her daughter said, "I was sleeping last night, and I was woken up by you." I said, "Oh that's funny, I saw you too! I didn't say anything because I thought I had just imagined it. I woke up, and the minute I opened my eyes you were floating straight towards me." It freaked Camille out when both of us told her the same story. Worried and concerned, she said, "I must have been astral traveling, but I don't remember doing it."

As a child, we never went to church, but my Mom's upbringing was always rooted in the Roman Catholic beliefs and religion. She attended Catholic boarding schools throughout her life. She did not believe in mediums or the spiritual. My Dad, an Atheist, didn't believe in God. Even my Grandmother, much later in life, became a devout Catholic nun for a time. Growing up, I had a very close friend who tried to convert me to becoming a Jehovah Witness. Noah, too, was Anglican. Needless to say, I have always kept an open mind.

I became quite close with Camille, my mother-in-law and, out of curiosity, joined her development circle. It was during one of these sessions, that I had an overwhelming spiritual event so profound, that I not only treasure it to this day but am thankful I was able to experience.

During the development circle, Camille encouraged us to meditate. I sat closing my eyes trying to clear my mind, and while doing my best to focus, I became instantaneously enveloped in a white light; no longer in my physical body. I was infused and immersed as one with the light. I was filled entirely with a sense of pure, absolute, and unconditional love. A euphoria so great, it embodied me, and there was nothing but love - no pain, no worry, no sorrow, no guilt, and no remorse. There was no concept of time, and it felt like an eternity. A timeless, exhilarating moment that took my breath away, and I gasped in awe. It was too beautiful to describe, and words were not enough to explain this true miracle. It was at this precise moment I knew without a doubt there was so much more to life that could not be explained by science or religion; above all, it was universal. I did not want to leave and, if at all possible, would have stayed in this comforting, indescribable sanctity. Whenever I need to rejuvenate, I remember this time and cherish it.

When I went to court to testify, Melanie made herself known. I walked into the courthouse and waited in the hall until they called my name. The overhead lights running the length of the hallway were flickering continuously. I remarked to Helen, "What's wrong with the lights?" Pointing; I asked, "Look, can't you see it?" She was oblivious to what I was talking about, and I continued to watch the parade of lights flickering in a steady, directional pattern. Try as I might, I could not rationalize or justify this bizarre occurrence, and, without warning, I sensed Melanie's presence. I knew she was there to help, and the comfort calmed my nerves.

While living in Cloverdale, I was feeling quite despondent over my struggle to get pregnant. I spent the day resting on the couch wallowing in self-pity and hopelessness. A force of someone taking their fist and punching the couch directly above me broke my reverie. Startled, I instantly heard in my head, "Stop feeling sorry for yourself!" The fear alone was enough for me to snap out of my quandary, and I took his warning as an implied deterrent. Spooked and jittery, it took several minutes before I could calm myself. Settling down, I realized, "He's right - I am feeling sorry for myself," and I regained my resolve not to give up. Again, I knew without a doubt that it was Noah's Dad.

Another memorable experience was with our dog, Brandy, a 14-year-old black lab cross we had since she was a puppy. We adopted her from the SPCA and, the moment we saw her, we knew she was the one. We were lucky though because at the same time another couple came in wanting to adopt her as well. He told us, "You'll have to draw names, and whosoever's name gets picked will get the puppy." Discouraged, we were quite impressed when the other couple backed away and said, "Okay, if you want her, we'll give in, and you can have her."

At 14-years-old, diagnosed with cancer; A fast spreading cancer, Brandy's health deteriorated quickly. Towards the end, we slept downstairs with her on our makeshift bed as she couldn't climb the stairs anymore.

One night, I woke up after shouting her name and reached out to her. She was whimpering and, as I peered into her eyes, I knew the time had come to take her in to get euthanized. While the shot was getting administered, I cradled her in my arms, stroked her, and whispered goodbye. The days after were filled with anguish, crying, and the insurmountable pain of missing her.

Three nights later, Brandy appeared in my dream. Conveying her thoughts telepathically, she said, "I've come to say goodbye." Teeming with happiness at the mere sight of her, I bent down to stroke her as I relished our precious time together. A few minutes later, she turned her head as if someone was calling out to her, and said, "I have to go now." With a last goodbye, she turned, retreated, and vanished into thin air. A sense of peace so profound engulfed me, and I realized I could let her go now knowing she was okay. I was extremely grateful to have had this chance at a final goodbye.

I would have a similar experience at the loss of my Grandfather. After my Grandfather had a second heart attack, my Mom and I went to Bellevue, Washington to be with him at the hospital. Unresponsive and incoherent, the doctors said there was nothing to be done; he was dying. Staying at a motel, the second night, I would have a dream so vivid I could recall every detail. My Grandfather appeared in our room, having passed directly through the wall. My Grandfather telepathically said, "I'm here to say goodbye, thank you for coming, and please tell your mother goodbye." With a solemn expression, he turned, walked through the wall again, and vanished. It wasn't long before he lapsed into a coma and hence was taken off life support.

Time elapsed with no further episodes to do with the other side. It seemed to come in stages relative to certain events occurring in my life.

I'm going off topic a little bit right now but, nevertheless, I need to tell of the strange experience Noah had while teaching first aid. Being a certified instructor, he taught in his spare time and, one day, arrived at New Westminster Secondary School to teach an evening class. He had never been to this school, even when he was younger - and yet, the moment he entered, he knew exactly where to go. He said, "I had the weirdest feeling like I had been there before, and I knew where everything was - talk about déjà vu," and his retelling of his experience gave me the goosebumps. I couldn't relate as I have never experienced déjà vu.

Victor, my second stepfather, died of lung failure in May 2010. Tess and I flew to Montreal for the funeral, as well as my brother on a separate flight. My Mom and Victor had moved to Montreal, and purchased a house together with Helen and her husband, Martin. The first night, we arrived late into the night and, after catching up, decided to turn in around 1:00 a.m., their time.

I took the couch on the main floor in the living room, Tess took the couch up on the third floor, and Billy slept in the guest room on the second floor. Upon entering the house, you came into the main foyer, with the living room on the left. The comfortable space of the living room adorned with a leather couch alongside the adjoining interior entry wall and supplemented by two leather chairs placed on each side of the front windows. Opposite the couch, a well-crafted, superb fireplace that carried into a formal dining room, right off the kitchen at the back of the house. To the right of the front door, the unique, traditionally designed staircase leading upstairs, and an adjoining den at the base of the stairs. From the entryway, the hallway led to the breakfast nook and family room combination to the right off the kitchen. The second floor consisted of the sleeping quarters, with the guest bedroom directly to the right of the stairs, the master bedroom (Helen and Martin's room), to the left, and my Mom's bedroom, kitty corner. Victor had a separate bedroom opposite my Mom's due to his deteriorating health issues. Having been diagnosed with diabetes, he eventually ended up having his leg amputated, and fitted with a prosthesis. He never bounced back and dealt with further medical problems. The third-floor layout contained an open, sectioned recreation room.

Everyone retired to bed, and I stretched out on the couch. I was wound up from the day's comings and goings; I was having trouble sleeping. The stillness was interrupted by someone milling about in the family room. I assumed somebody had got up and come downstairs. When I looked though, I saw the house was dark, and no lights were on. Closing my eyes, every sound I heard magnified. First, the sound of someone fiddling with something, then walking over to the back door and checking the lock. Then, proceed through the breakfast nook/family room, and traipse down the hall. The couch positioned so that the back of the couch was facing the front hallway, and I couldn't see past the couch into the hallway. With no apparent explanation, apprehension crept in at this anomaly. A moment later, I could sense someone peering over the top of the couch and became certain of the fact that it was

Victor. I froze in fear, held my breath, pretended to be asleep, and kept my eyes closed tightly. I daresay, I was terrified! In that very same instance, I could sense Victor stop, gaze over the back of the couch, give a nod of approval after checking to see that I was all settled in, and then he turned and walked away. He proceeded to the front door, and I could hear him checking the lock. He then made his way to the stairs and stopped. A bang resonated through the quiet, and it was loud enough that I was surprised no one woke up. Unable to discern the bang, a moment later, I heard him starting up the stairs. To clarify, as I already mentioned, Victor had his leg amputated so what I heard was a step, and then a thump, all the way up the stairs. At the top of the landing, he stopped again. A few minutes later, I heard water running, and then it went quiet.

Petrified, I did not budge. I debated going upstairs to wake someone up, but I was too afraid of running into Victor. I finally forced myself to move as I desperately had to go to the bathroom. I managed to get up my nerve and, in a quick dash, made it to the bathroom, and switched on the light. Panic-stricken, my heart racing a mile a minute, I tried to settle my nerves by taking in deep breaths. I could not believe what was going on, and I was beside myself. I reasoned, "Calm down, and be rational." All I could think of was, "I've gotta take a sleeping pill, then, maybe I can fall asleep, and this will all be over." Nervously, with my heart pounding out of my chest, I darted back to the couch, closed my eyes, and tried to calm down. All at once, I sensed Victor standing in the living room. In that brief moment the atmosphere changed, the air was lighter it seemed, and a peacefulness settled over the room; not like before. I knew then Victor was gone - he only returned to say goodbye, and he had now moved on. The comforting ambiance permeated the room, and I wasn't scared anymore.

In the morning, I relayed the extraordinary happenings to my Mom once she came down. She didn't believe me, but I didn't care. I was insistent, and step by step I told her what I'd heard. She confirmed Victor's nightly routine, of which I hadn't known. He was always the last one to bed, and he would check to make sure the doors were locked, and the lights were off. The part of stopping at the bottom of the stairs, was him reaching for his cane to make his way upstairs. The step and thump on the stairs were of him using his cane. At the landing on top of the stairs, he would turn his walker around, which he parked at the top of the stairs, and would use it to get to his room. She said, "He always went to his bathroom before bedtime, and used the sink to wash up." That's why I heard the water running. My Mom's only comment was, "Why didn't he come to me?" I said, "He probably did, but you were sleeping. I'm really surprised you didn't wake up with all the noise. I didn't drop it and kept talking about my experience as I felt Mom needed to know. Even though she didn't believe in the spiritual, I had to let her know that Victor had come to say goodbye. Mom finally asked, "If this is so, why would you be scared if you knew it was Victor?" and, dumbstruck, I answered, "Because he's dead!" Needless to say, I didn't sleep by myself the rest of my stay. After contemplating this eccentricity, I wondered how on earth was I able to hear with such clarity every movement, every step, irrespective of where Victor was in the house. I could only equate it to being in a vortex and caught up in this void all you could differentiate were the sounds coming from within.

In 2011, Nick, my nephew-in-law, died by suicide. At 36-years-old, he had paranoid schizophrenia since the age of eighteen. Attending the Celebration of Life service, I listened to the eulogy and the rendition of Nick playing his guitar to a piece of music by Jimi Hendrix. An overwhelming urge to start clapping my hands overcame me and, at the same time, I sensed Camille, my mother-in-law, right behind me ushering me up to make a speech. I tried to shrug it off as I am not good at public speaking, but the urge was too strong to resist. Whether I liked it or not, Camille was going to make sure I didn't back out. As soon as the rendition ended, the Minister asked if anyone wanted to say a few words. With apprehension, I stood up and tentatively approached the front. Very uncomfortable and embarrassed, I thought, "I don't know what to say - I didn't rehearse this, and I sure didn't expect to be giving a speech. Oh well, I have no choice - Camille is making sure of that." I spoke to how much Nick meant to me, how proud I was of him, and the person he was. At the end and, again out of my control, the undeniable urge to clap my hands was overwhelming. Here we go, and as I started clapping my hands, everyone in Church stood up and joined in. Afterward, I got the distinct impression that I needed to do this for Nick, for him to know how much everyone loved him. As for Camille, my mother-in-law, she died in 2008, three years earlier, from Alzheimer's. A long-drawn-out illness, she suffered through the devastating stages of this disease. During Nick's eulogy, it would be the first time she had made herself known to me that I was conscious of - a heartfelt moment, as it was a blessing to feel her presence and, yet at the same time, I was wrought with a degree of sadness as I missed her so much.

It wasn't until I had cancer that the spiritual awakening would erupt full-blown. As I've said before, I received no support or encouragement other than from Noah and was still struggling with the hurt and rejection.

One late afternoon, while lying on the couch, a white orb materialized in front of the living room window. Approximately 1m in diameter, it floated and was stationery. Searching for a plausible explanation, I rationalized, "Maybe it's coming from outside, and shining through the blinds, but I noticed the blinds closed." Determined to solve this dilemma, I thought, "If it is coming through the blinds from outside, there would only be light filtering in through the slats." The orb was solid, stayed for more than a fleeting moment, and then disappeared.

I had gone to church one Sunday morning, a spiritualist church in New Westminster that I'd been to before. Not long into the service, I observed luminescent flickers of light darting throughout the room - a steady array of "dancing" to and fro that no one else seemed to be aware of since the service was proceeding as usual. When the spiritual healing part of the service got under way, I sat mesmerized as a continuous burst of white light (very much like a strobe light) pulsed forth into my forehead. I didn't know what to make of it and, not knowing, I sat absorbed in wonder. Honored, I was quite sure I was receiving some form of healing from the other side. I would have much more signs of spirits showing they were near and took great comfort in knowing I wasn't alone. Going outside to water the garden one morning, I turned the hose on, letting it spray into the yard until the water turned cold. Coming out of nowhere, a hummingbird hovered about 2.5m directly in front of where I stood. We locked eyes, and there seemed to be a deep connection. This hummingbird wasn't of the typical variety - it was more colorful and surpassed a span of 20cm in length from wing to wing. I have never seen a hummingbird of this size, this species, and have only ever seen it once.

Another time, Melanie's favorite song, "The Lion Sleeps Tonight," came on the radio. It had been years since I'd heard this song, and it brought a smile to my face. A few times, I would smell perfume like the sweet aroma of flowers. Struck by the strong aroma, I checked for the source, but once again I couldn't find it. An afterthought occurred, "It smells just like the perfume Camille used to wear," and as soon as I acknowledged it, it was gone.

I was waiting to receive an update on some test results and was feeling quite apprehensive on the drive to the hospital for my doctor's appointment. A sudden nudge on the back of my seat broke my reverie and, as it continued, I thought the truck was having mechanical problems. I kept looking around to determine the source and, as close as I could figure, it wasn't coming from the underside of the truck. Instead, it felt very similar to what Colin would do when he didn't have enough leg room, and he would resort to pushing his cramped knees into the back of my seat. It happened three times, and my gut told me, "Okay, someone is here keeping me company" and, intuitively, I knew Nick, my nephew-in-law, was there to keep me company. As soon as this thought came into my head, it stopped, and with it, I felt reassured.

Many times, I have experienced visions of family members who have passed. One instance, Camille and Nick appeared standing together smiling, and radiating with happiness - the difference being they were both younger, and not the age they had been when they passed. Nick, I could explain as I had known him since he was the age of three, but

Camille I didn't meet until she was in her late fifties. By Camille's appearance, I estimated her to be in her thirties and was much younger than when I knew her. Another time, it would be Victor and, once more, a younger version, but easily recognizable.

Have you ever wondered how it would be to find your soul mate or have a kindred spirit - someone you feel a deep connection to, and are joined by sharing a special bond that you are in sync with?

Not long ago, when I was going through my various stages of hurt and anger, I awoke from a dream and could recall every little detail down to a tee. In the dream, I spent the day in the companionship of this one woman, as only best friends would do. I knew this woman, the strong connection was apparent and, yet, she was not someone I was familiar with in real life - the bond was so strong, it felt as if we were kindred spirits, and the closeness was there with no effort needed. There was no struggle - we clicked, were in harmony, and enjoyed each other's company. She wasn't anyone I recognized who I could put my finger on and, yet in this dream, I did know her. I was puzzled as I tried to figure out who this woman could be. The dream brought forth a comfort, a sense of acceptance, and a friendship unparalleled to anything I knew in my lifetime. A few nights later, I awoke to this same woman calling my name. She materialized standing beside my bed, and her face projected a look of concern and worry. Answering her, now completely alert, I read her thoughts. She wanted me to stop acting so angrily; it wasn't doing me any good. I wondered again who this woman could be, and then it struck me! It was Julie Johnson; I was sure of it! She was Melanie's best friend and had become close with all of us, as well as her sister Lacey. After Melanie had died, we remained close, and it was her family I moved in with when I first met Noah. I had lost touch after moving out, and learned years later, while she was in her thirties she hit her head while getting into the bathtub, which caused her accidental death. At the time, my sisters went to Julie's funeral, and Tess commented on how much she had changed in appearance. After talking with Lacey, Tess learned that Melanie had told Julie about my Dad sexually abusing her. Melanie made Julie promise not to tell, and she kept her word - she didn't tell. I wasn't able to identify Julie as the last time I had seen her, was when she was around the age of sixteen. It finally dawned on me; it was her bangs that gave it away. She always parted her bangs in the middle and wore them to each side. Some habits never change, and, like a cowlick, her bangs worn in the same manner as before.

I have to say with all that has happened; I feel privileged and blessed. I do not take these experiences for granted and appreciate and hold on to them for emotional support. I have received more help from the other side, for which I feel gratitude. Every so often it comes and with it the support and comfort to let me know I'm not alone.

Out walking Abby, our Golden Retriever, one afternoon, a thought popped into my head. It was strong enough to pay attention to - the thought, "Noah needs to do first aid." I shrugged it off, but a day later Noah said, "It's really weird - I've seen Trauma First Aid vehicles everywhere I go today. It made me think about getting back into first aid." Noah used to teach for Trauma First Aid. It was with this comment, I replied, "That's funny – yesterday, right out of the blue, it popped into my head, you're supposed to be doing first aid. I couldn't shrug it off as the feeling was so strong." Noah waved it aside, and commented, "It's probably nothing; I'll think about it." I persisted, and told Noah, "Get back into first aid - get out of electrical and do first aid. That's what you're supposed to be doing." With Noah's lack of response, I let it drop but, a week or so later, the strong urge was back. This time, I asked Noah, "Have you thought any more about first aid?" Noah gave more excuses and then replied, "No, I'm going to forget about it. I'm too old." I argued with him and insisted he needed to take it seriously. I said, "They haven't told me this for nothing, and it came back a second time - so you have to pay attention." It was enough of a push to get Noah motivated. For the past year, Noah has been busy renewing his instructor's first aid courses, and teaching. His intention is to get back into teaching first aid full-time; that's his goal, and we both know that is what he is meant to do.

The fortitude, the resolve, comes in waves. The struggle, insecurity, and the unknown are constant. It would be nice to think that help from the other side would be forthcoming on a regular basis, but I guess that would defeat the purpose of free will and learning. It is our responsibility to take what we have, had been given, and better ourselves through perseverance.

Sixteen

Going with my gut has got me out of a few mishaps more than once, and I'm so glad I didn't ignore it or just shrug it off.

I remember driving back from Washington, USA. Noah, Helen, and I were on the freeway, and I had a sudden, terrible urge to stop. I pulled over to the shoulder and said to Noah, "I don't know what's the matter; for some reason, I can't drive. I have a strong feeling that something's going to happen, and I can't shake it off." After only a couple of minutes, unable to shake the feeling of dread, I said to Noah, "I think you should drive." We started off and, sure enough, a few minutes later, a speeding car veered out of control just ahead of us. Noah had a split second to swerve and prevent a crash; imagine - broadsided, seriously injured or killed if I hadn't pulled over when I did. If it hadn't been for Noah's fast reflexes, and my decision to stop, I don't think we would have been able to avoid the disaster.

When we were living on SW Marine Drive in Vancouver, B.C., we rented the top floor of a house, and other tenants occupied the basement level. As you entered through the side entrance, you came into a dimly lit hallway with a small bedroom on the right and, further down, a bathroom on the left. At the end of the hallway was the kitchen and, as you turned the corner, it led into the living room. Wooden French patio doors opened out onto a spacious outside wooden deck. At work, one day, a sudden and intense feeling of dread came over me, and I knew for some inexplicable reason I had to get home. Leaving work early, I could not rid myself of the foreboding fear that something was wrong. With an uneasy feeling, I unlocked the side door and wondered why Brandy didn't come and greet me. The quiet, empty hallway was disquieting, and I quizzically called out to Brandy. Growing impatient at her defiant behavior, I went looking for her. Our bedroom door was closed, which was odd, and as I opened the door, I found Brandy cowering on the bed. I noticed she was scared and visibly shaking. I thought maybe she had pushed the door closed by accident and got stuck in the bedroom. As I called her to come, she wouldn't move off the bed. Puzzled, I went and checked the rest of the house. The sight of all our furniture gone stopped me in my tracks; somebody robbed us! The police came out to file a report, and dust for fingerprints. Upon further questioning, they informed us that the tenant below had a warrant out for his arrest. The police said, "We've been looking for this guy for quite some time. More than likely, he was the one who broke in" and, pointing to the smashed pane of the French glass doors said, "He knew your routine." With that, I thought, "That would explain the day they came upstairs for a friendly chat." Taking an interest, they asked if we were all settled in, and used this time to comment on how nice everything looked while casing our place. Moreover, they were overly attentive towards Brandy. I'm certain my timing was such that I must have interrupted their break-in or cut it short, but I was sure glad they left Brandy alone and didn't hurt her. That was why she was in the bedroom with the door closed - they locked her in while they were busy emptying out our place!

While living at the same place, the second episode of foreboding took place when I took Brandy for a walk at Rumble Park. A routine, I headed for the secluded trail that ran behind an industrial park, as I had done so many times before. As soon as I reached the log laid out at the start of the trail, I stopped dead in my tracks. A foreboding came over me and, looking ahead, I had an overwhelming sense of dread, and the trail seemed menacing. I turned abruptly and made my way to the open area on the other side. Still quite nervous and afraid, I couldn't shake the feeling, and I didn't stay long. A couple of days later, while watching the news report, a woman has been sexually assaulted; the same trail and the assailant had been hiding in the bushes. The police issued a warning not to use this trail as the suspect was still at large. Goosebumps ran through my entire body as I thought, "that could have been me."

Another time, I would be driving home on Kingsway Street near Central Park. It was late, around 3:00 a.m., when a pickup truck came barreling up behind me at an astonishing rate of speed. Startled, I jumped and, as he passed on the left, I gave him a blast of my horn. Not the smartest thing to do, as I was soon to find out. Up ahead, he made a U-turn right in the middle of the street and, heading straight for me, gunned it. The streets were barren as it was so early, and he continued his deliberate game of chicken. Scared, I tried to get the attention of the first car driving by, and as she slowed, I screamed, "Help, he's trying to kill me." She drove away in fear. On his third attempt, he once again barreled down upon me. Approaching lightning fast and, with no time to waste, I jerked my wheel to the right to avoid the impending crash. The moment of chance and the timing couldn't have been more precise. Miraculously, I had turned exactly at the location where a pull-in abutted the street. I didn't even know it was there! Before he had a chance to return, I sped as fast as I could to get away. Shaking uncontrollably, I turned off Kingsway and prayed he wasn't going to come back for more. I called the police, and when they arrived, I gave my report and his description. About a week or so later, I was at a restaurant on Kingsway, and I couldn't believe this same individual happened to be the cook. I quickly phoned the police and was promptly told we can't do anything; even though I had identified him, they would not allow a partial ID as my original description was of him sitting in his truck. I guess this time he got away with it, and he was off the hook.

Living in Mission, my morning routine was to let Blackjack outside at around 4:30 to 5:00 a.m. before leaving for work. This one morning, while getting ready for work, I heard a long, drawn-out meow of a cat in agony. I went to the sliding door, opened it, and called Blackjack. He didn't come and worried I said to Noah, "I have a feeling something has happened to Blackjack. We need to find him." A few minutes later, I went out the front door to go and search for Blackjack, and to my shock, a coyote was strolling down the middle of our street.

Our eyes locked, and the look he gave was one of contempt at having lost a meal. Spending the next hour or so searching for Blackjack, he finally came out of hiding and lay crouching at the sliding door. Reaching out to pick him up, I could see he was in shock and severe pain. Gently checking him over, I noticed several puncture wounds in his head. I was certain of the fact that I must have interrupted the coyote's attack when I opened our sliding door and, the coyote surprised and taken off guard, was enough to allow Blackjack time to escape his clutches. Rushing Blackjack to the Emergency Veterinarian, we were told he was one lucky cat. With all the injuries - a dislocated jaw and deep puncture wounds to his head, they were amazed he had survived.

Another aspect, divine intervention has gotten us out of a few close calls: the time Noah was driving his motorcycle to work. It was in the middle of winter, and he was on Westminster Highway following slowly behind a steady stream of traffic. The road conditions were slick and icy as it had snowed during the night. Up ahead, a chain reaction as cars slammed into each other unable to stop. Noah watched as they plowed into each other like dominoes. Noah avoided the impending crash by turning abruptly and driving alongside the road on the slightest edge beside the ditch. He said, "I got goosebumps, and I couldn't believe it! Every time I passed a car, I watched as one by one, in slow motion, the cars piled up. His quick reflexes and the split-second timing kept him safe and unharmed.

Another time, we were all headed to Sylvan Lake for a dinner party. It was the middle of winter, and the highway from Edmonton was hazardous. Getting caught in a sudden snowstorm, we had to contend with the blowing snow, and the visibility was poor. Conditions treacherous, we slowed down. Blinding lights broke our concentration as, out of nowhere, a semi-truck came barreling down upon us. I watched in paralyzing fear as I knew there was absolutely no way the semi-truck could avoid smashing into us as he was coming up too fast. With my eyes focused on the side mirror, I screamed and gripped the seat waiting for the impending impact. As if in slow motion, I watched the semi-truck abruptly turn his wheel to the right, heedlessly speed past us, and barge through the piled high snowbank on the shoulder without slowing down. I honestly did not know how the semi-truck hadn't lost control and avoided disaster. Noah and I sat in utter disbelief and were shocked at how close we had all come to dying.

With divine intervention, the coincidences are such you can't ignore. Subtle signs that happen quite unexpectedly and are inexplicable.

Noah was admitted to Lions Gate Hospital with pneumonia when he was three years old. His condition critical, the doctors informed Noah's Mom and Dad that Noah wasn't expected to last through the night. They said, "If you want to call in a priest, we would suggest you do it now." Even in the state Noah was in, he recalled the priest standing beside his bed, praying for him, and giving him his last rights. The next day, Noah's health improved, and his recovery was miraculous.

Noah had lost contact with his older sister, Carolyn and, after years of trying to find her whereabouts, our efforts to locate her went nowhere. One day, I was looking for something and was rummaging through boxes stored away. Sorting through a pile of papers I was holding; a letter dropped out by chance. Curious, I opened it up. It was the last letter we had received from Carolyn, which I hadn't even known I'd kept. Noting the address, we searched the internet and hit another dead end. In the letter, there was mention of a town in Scotland, and I said to Noah, "Look up this town - maybe she moved there." A long shot, but I thought, "We're not having any luck finding her anywhere else." It was such a coincidence when, a few keystrokes later, a website about Noah's niece, Sandy, popped up. Sending an e-mail to ensure we had the right person, it wasn't long before we were in contact with her. It was funny as they were now living in Ontario!

Seventeen

Noah and I live our lives without the preconceived notion that we are entitled. We keep a low profile. I'm viscerally irritated by people who can't stop talking about themselves, who think they are better than everyone else. We do not try and prove our worth. So many times, people are more interested in material possessions and climbing the ladder to acquire power and prestige. It's not for us, and we are consciously quiet and unassuming. I was unable to work due to my cancer, has put a financial strain on us, but it has opened our eyes. The hectic lifestyle just isn't worth it, and you come to realize what's important in life, and that is spending time together.

Noah and I have accomplished a lot. We are not wealthy by any means but manage. Patience is not our strongest virtue, but we have endured. In the end, we are the winners as you can't replace love.

We are constantly underestimated only for the fact that we do not talk about ourselves or look for confrontation. I stick up for what is right for it's a matter of principle. I will not allow the negative criticisms, slander or the blame not now - I vocalize, thereby assumptions are not made or misunderstood as they have been in the past.

Noah, starting in the military, was quite a marksman and asked if he wanted a career as a sniper. He joined the Volunteer Fire Department and later became a Certified First Aid Instructor. A couple of his past achievements included teaching Industrial First Aid at Simon Fraser University, a First Aid Attendant in the movie industry and, during filming, filling in as a movie extra. In electrical wholesale, he started in the warehouse and worked his way up through the ranks to become a Branch Manager. More recently, he went back into teaching first aid and renewing his Instructor's First Aid Certificate.

The times he would be dispatched to the Fire Department: a baby dying of SIDS (Sudden Infant Death Syndrome), where he tried so hard to resuscitate. Fires, one at the mill, where he pulled an all-nighter. Pedestrian fatalities, when he hosed up the macabre remains from the street after an unfortunate soul got struck by a car. Once driving the firetruck and attending a call by himself as no one else showed up.

Timing and good fortune have not been in our favor. We do not seem to have luck on our side. Noah's favorite saying is, "If we didn't have bad luck, we wouldn't have any luck at all." What we have, we have acquired through hard work and persistence.

Limitations in place, we both did not have the financial backing of our family. We started from scratch and, for the most part, on our own.

Eighteen

The timing of cancer, and with Logan and Colin having turned 14 years old, truly impacted me. The realization that I might die seemed to have opened up and brought to the surface every moment of my life. With no choice, I was facing the responsibility of reviewing my life.

I have been able to let go of the past, leave it behind, and move ahead. I had a lot to look forward to and always had time. Now it seems with cancer, I've had to re-evaluate, and reflect on my life.

Colin and Logan, turning 14 years old, sent me on an emotional roller coaster ride. All the old memories flooded back, and I would look at Colin and Logan and imagine at this age Melanie was dead by suicide. The enormity of my past hit me like a ton of bricks - finally seeing, able to identify through my own children's lives, the extremity of circumstances we had endured. I took this time to tell Colin and Logan about Melanie, my Dad, Lucas, and Matt. I told them both, "trust and respect must be earned." I wanted them to know if they ever needed to talk, I was here. No matter what, we could always work it out, and never to give up.

My Mom did not appreciate the fact I told Colin and Logan about my childhood. She had hoped it would have stayed in the past, been buried, and thrown under the rug once more. I was empathetic, and understood she was only trying to start anew with her grandchildren, while I thought, "I'm not doing this to hurt you but, from this point on, there will be no more secrets."

I have always found it hard to trust, and words mean nothing to me. As the adage goes, "actions speak louder than words." I miss my mother-in-law, Camille, every day. Everyone thinks that blood is thicker than water – but with us it was not so. She was a special person in my life, whom I admired, someone I could look up to, and respect. She always gave a helping hand to anyone in need. I remember her ways, her outlook on life, and her devotion. Many times I hear her say, "Don't mind me, I have a few screws loose." Laughing, she would reach up to her head and remark, "Hold on, I just have to tighten up the screws;" her actions implying, "Take me as I am."

I look back on my life and say, "I'd do it all over again if it got me to where I am," and, "It's made me who I am." I don't take anything for granted, don't complain as I have Noah, my soul mate, and Colin and Logan, our miracles in life. I owe my life to Noah as he is by my side. It hasn't always been easy; we've made our mistakes, and had our differences too, but we compromise and talk it through. In December 2017, it will be 38 years since we were married - need I say more!? Love and respect are two of the most important factors in facing conflict and resolution. Without love and respect, there is no compromise - there's only control.

I have tried to live my life helping others, and to an extent put the needs of others before myself. It's not for monetary gain; I do it for free and do not expect a payback or something in return. That is the difference - I give of my time because I want to, not because I must. I am not phony and, what you see, is what you get.

I learned out of necessity two important lessons in life from my Mom and Dad – mainly, how to be independent and hard working. Remember the phrase, "You won't have everything handed to you on a silver platter."

At the same time, I can turn the bad into good. Too many people stay in a slump, act the victim, without taking it and turning it around. Living in the past, they blame others for their misfortune. I have learned life is what you make of it. Sitting back, and feeling sorry for yourself, will not bring about change. Sitting on the sidelines and waiting for it will not work either. You need to go and get it! The struggle is there, the path not always clear but, in the end, the result is one of gratitude and fulfillment.

I will not repeat the cycle of physical and mental abuse, and the criticism and negativity; I stayed strong. I encourage Colin and Logan to do their best and be proud of who they are. At around the age of 14, we had a lot of problems with Logan, and he was acting out big time. His temper would flare, and he would become defiant about his schoolwork. The contention wasn't helping when the shouting matches ensued. It finally reached a point where I knew I had to stop screaming, stop arguing - it wasn't helping, and was making it far worse. I needed to find out why Logan was acting this way as it was so much out of character. I sat him down, and calmly asked why he was acting like this. It took a bit - a lot of listening, to get to the root of the problem. It turns out; he thought he wasn't as good as Colin, and from there it had steamrolled. We were able to resolve it positively. I told him, "Logan, you are you, and Colin is Colin. Stop comparing yourself and be proud of who you are." Most of all, not to let the stigma of being a twin bring about the competition and judging yourself by the other. Instead, to be your own person, an individual.

In the case of Tess and me, she always tried to outdo me. The competition is something I prefer to do without and wish she would take her initiative. It's difficult being an identical twin as it's assumed we are tied together as one - that our lives, our interests, our likes, and our talents must be equal and parallel. I'm so tired of hearing from Mom, "Have you talked to Tess?" only because she is my twin. She doesn't say this about Helen and Billy.

Logan and Colin are now 17 years old, and it is incredible how quickly time passes. At this age it's hard to imagine that I met Noah and, even more, astonishing to think at the age of nineteen, we married.

I continue to live by Camille's proverbs, "As another door closes, another will open"; this is my outlook - I still have more to do and, God willing, I will. No matter the challenge I have faced, I push on knowing change always comes in time.

I think everyone can agree time is the only component of change. To a certain extent, you cannot continue blaming your past for at one point or another, it's your own choices, and what you do with them that determine your destiny. Knowledge is not gained by saying, "if only, if only." You cannot change the past. Instead, you take your experiences and grow from them striving all the while. I'm not perfect, but who is? And it's certainly not easy but, whoever said it would be? I'd rather be moving ahead though than standing still. At least when you are moving you are getting closer to where you're going. I do not hold grudges; life is too short. Instead, I choose to remember the good as well as the bad because, in the end, it only affects me in what I do and accomplish in life.

I look to the future and, in writing this book, I close the door on this chapter of my life. I want people to like me for who I am. I think that is why I have never talked about my past, till now. I do not want my past remembered; I don't want pity or sympathy for what I have gone through and do not want to be known as a victim. I want people to remember me for now, at present, for my achievements, and the good I have done. Everyone has their struggles, and for whatever reason this is mine. You may not agree with every aspect I have written, but that is your right. I only know I've spent too much time feeling insecure, not worthy enough, too afraid of what people thought of me, and it held me back. I can only say now, "think what you will, don't judge, and accept me for who I am. Whether you agree or not, is your prerogative."

One night, as a final step in healing, I had a vision of such absolute clarity. Tt was monumental. I was standing at the end of a long, brightly lit hallway. Immaculately clean, the walls were pure white, and the floor glistened like glass. The corridor lined with several closed doors on each side. As I glanced down the hallway, the sight of Boris interrupted and invaded this pristine space. I was gripped by a paralyzing fear as I watched as him walk nonchalantly towards me.

His demeanor was infallible; his stealth was one of marked determination. The grin plastered on his face gave a prelude to his excitement and thrill of coming to get me once more. It was a moment so real that, at first, reverted to my past, back to my inner child, and was too afraid to move. Once he drew near, I transformed and was not the child anymore. I screamed with conviction, "Get away from me!" I awoke to feel omniscient; the clarity took hold, and a sense of finality to never again be under his control. I had broken free, and free will was mine to take.

In writing this book, I wanted to give a special tribute to Melanie. She fought with immense fortitude until she could take no more. I just wish she could have known that suicide was not her only option. I wish I had seen the signs and been able to help - my only hope to convey that with any adversity, you can survive. In telling Melanie's story, it is not only to pay homage to her life but, in so doing, to save one person's life - and that I do for her.

Remember, let someone know you are getting abused. Talk, reach out, and don't stop until someone believes you and will help. The blame does not befall the child; it is not your fault under any circumstances. The tragedy is, not one of us knew how to express ourselves or open the lines of communication, and it was a learned behavior we all became accustomed to – the shocking truth, and the revelation was that all of us were unaware. With the dysfunction, we were unable to obtain a healthy relationship, and even the separate ties that bind Mother/Daughter, Sister/Sister, Sister/Brother and so on, did not exist. We all paid the price and suffered the outcome.

Most of all, do not give up. Believe in good; this is your lifeline, it makes you strong, and with it follows the choice to overcome. I got through the sexual abuse by believing in good and, by holding onto the good, I had the inner strength to endure and overcome the demoralizing and detrimental effects of incest. So many times, throughout my life, if I had listened to what people said, I would have given up: thirteen years trying to get pregnant, the odds stacked against us, and told we would never have children. The plight of fighting through cancer, the misdiagnosis, and the ongoing battle for life. Our resolve, one step at a time, and with it the simple fact that it only takes one - one person to change a life, one moment in time to change a life, and one good deed to change a life. Miracles are all around us, and what we do impacts each one of us, as we are all connected.

Live your life by example, and don't let the stress of your tedious routine of your daily life have precedence over your choices and outlook. When in doubt, I reflect back on Camille's development circle, where I was immersed and infused with the white light - the euphoria so great, it embodied me, and there was nothing but love: no pain, no worry, no sorrow, no guilt, and no remorse. This comforting, indescribable sanctity of universal truth is what I hold on to, and it washes away all doubt. Let the simple things in life guide you, and don't give up on hope.

In summary, my only wish is you take a little piece of what you've read and move forward with a renewed sense of hope and well-being. Take the time just to be there, to help, as you never know what lays ahead. Life is just too short, and you know what? You DO count!

In ending, this is my turn, and it's my turn to talk. I have always let things go, never wanting to hurt anyone but, I know if it's the last thing I do, I will tell my side as it needs telling; this is my legacy, and maybe now you'll understand. Don't judge the book by its cover - just have a look inside.